Spelling Matters

3rd Edition

Andrew J Woods

Pearson Australia
(a division of Pearson Australia Group Pty Ltd)
707 Collins Street, Melbourne, Victoria 3008
PO Box 23360, Melbourne, Victoria 8012
www.pearson.com.au

First published 1993
Second edition 2002
Third edition 2008

2018 2017 2016 2015
13 12 11 10 9

Editor: Frith Luton
Text designer: Meaghan Barbuto
Typesetter: Anita Adams and Eugenio Fazio
Cover designer: Meaghan Barbuto
Cover illustration: Photolibrary Pty Ltd
Illustrations: Boris Silvestri
Prepress work by the Type Factory
Printed and bound in Australia by Pegasus Media & Logistics

Pearson Australia Group Pty Ltd ABN 40 004 245 943

Acknowledgements
The publishers wish to thank the following organisations who kindly gave permission to reproduce copyright material in this book:

A.A. Milne, excerpt from *When We Were Very Young* © The Trustees of the Pooh Properties. Published by Egmont UK Ltd London and used with permission: p. 49.

James Kirkup, excerpt from the poem 'The Lonely Scarecrow', 1963. Reprinted with permission from Curtis Brown as the Literary Agent for James Kirkup: p. 81.

John Masefield, excerpt from the poem 'Sea Fever'. Reprinted with permission from the Society of Authors as the Literary Representative of the Estate of John Masefield: pp. 15, 75.

Contents

Introduction

Welcome to *Spelling Matters Book* 5.

The *Spelling Matters* series has been developed to allow both the classroom teacher and the parent to improve the students' word attack skills and vocabulary range. The series provides exercises for use in the classroom and at home. This book contains 40 work units (36 Classroom and Home Study Units and four Review Units).

The Classroom Unit

At the beginning of each unit a list of words is provided. The words in this list have a phonological, visual, morphemic or etymological relationship to each other. The Classroom Unit is a series of exercises designed to develop phonological, visual and (in the Word Building section) morphemic knowledge. Challenge words are provided in each unit for vocabulary extension.

The Home Study Unit

The Home Study Unit should be completed at home, and parents are encouraged to assist their children with this unit.

The quotation, proverb, fact or rhyme shows how words from the lists have been used in our language.

The exercises in each Home Study Unit are similar in nature to those found in the Classroom Unit, although more word puzzle activities are provided.

Word Knowledge is aimed at further developing students' etymological knowledge and encourages experimentation with language.

The General Knowledge section provides opportunities to extend student understanding of related vocabulary. Students should be encouraged to seek help to complete this section if necessary, thereby involving parents directly in Home Study assignments. (Answers can be found at the end of this book.)

Self-assessment

Students are encouraged to assess their own progress by testing each other on a selection of List and Challenge words on the completion of each unit.

Provided at the back of the book is:

- a glossary of terms used in the units of work. These words are in **bold** in the text.
- a Spelling Reference List containing all the List and Challenge words used in the 40 units, which can be used by teachers, parents and students as another means of checking mastery of words.

A final note

Because language develops at different rates, students may not necessarily need to work at specified levels. Some teachers may wish to select isolated units of work related to a particular student's area of weakness.

Remember that spelling and vocabulary development should be associated with a variety of language experiences and should therefore be integrated into a total learning program.

Andrew Woods

How to use Spelling Matters

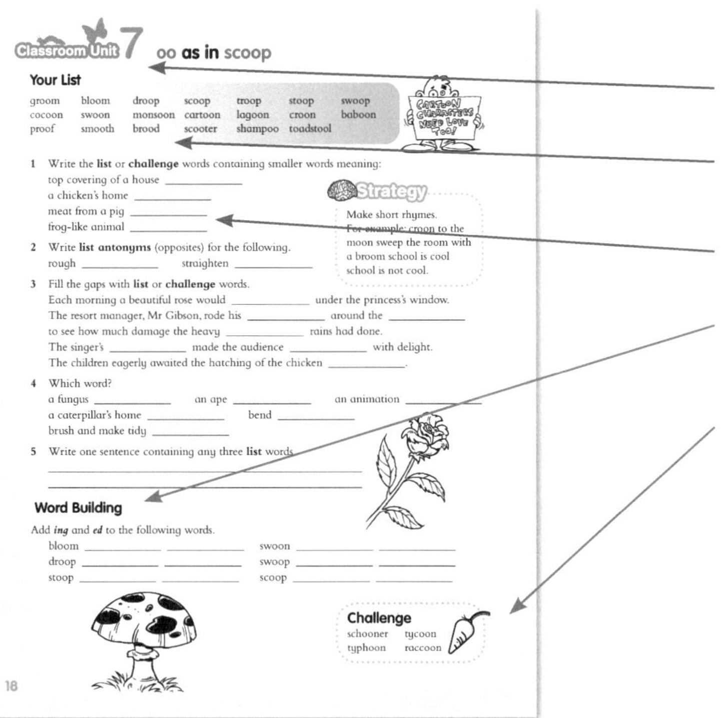

Classroom Unit 7 oo as in scoop

Your List

groom bloom droop scoop troop stoop swoop
cocoon swoon monsoon cartoon lagoon croon baboon
proof smooth brood scooter shampoo toadstool

1 Write the **list** or **challenge** words containing smaller words meaning:
top covering of a house ____________
a chicken's home ____________
meat from a pig ____________
frog-like animal ____________

2 Write **list antonyms** (opposites) for the following.
rough ____________ straighten ____________

3 Fill the gaps with **list** or **challenge** words.
Each morning a beautiful rose would ____________ under the princess's window.
The resort manager, Mr Gibson, rode his ____________ around the ____________
to see how much damage the heavy ____________ rains had done.
The singer's ____________ made the audience ____________ with delight.
The children eagerly awaited the hatching of the chicken ____________.

4 Which word?
a fungus ____________ an ape ____________ an animation ____________
a caterpillar's home ____________ bend ____________
brush and make tidy ____________

5 Write one sentence containing any three **list** words.

Strategy
Make short rhymes.
For example: croon to the moon sweep the room with a broom school is cool school is not cool.

Word Building

Add *ing* and *ed* to the following words.
bloom ____________ ____________ swoon ____________ ____________
droop ____________ ____________ swoop ____________ ____________
stoop ____________ ____________ scoop ____________ ____________

Challenge
schooner tycoon
typhoon raccoon

18

This is the Unit you must do at school.

Use this list of words to help you do the exercises.

Answer these questions by using the List words.

This will help you learn more about your List words.

Feel like a challenge? Learn the meanings of these words and how to spell them.

Can you find the List or Challenge word?

This work must be done at home.
Ask your parents to help you with it.

Try using the new words you find in this section when you next write a story, a letter, or in your diary or journal.

You may need to use reference books to help you with this section. Perhaps Mum, Dad or someone else could help.

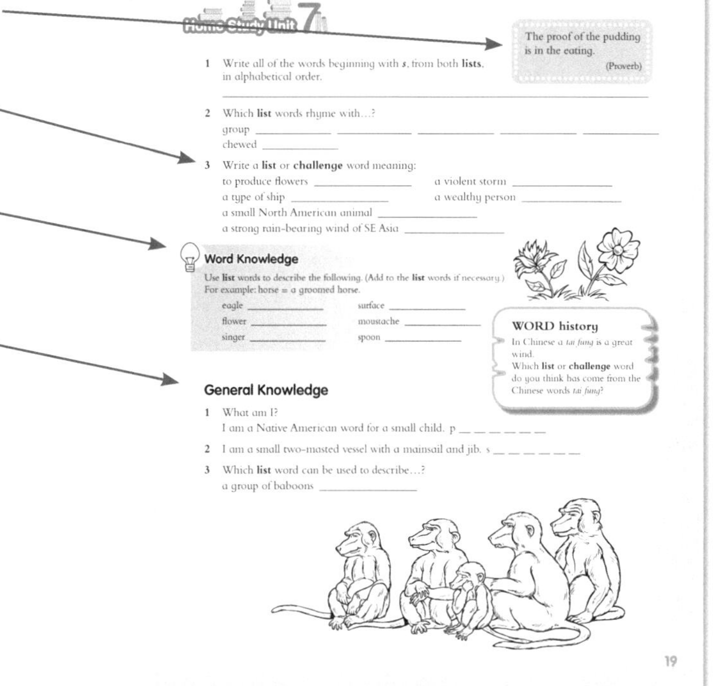

Home Study Unit 7

The proof of the pudding is in the eating. (Proverb)

1 Write all of the words beginning with *s*, from both **lists**, in alphabetical order.

2 Which **list** words rhyme with...?
group ____________ ____________ ____________ ____________ ____________
chewed ____________

3 Write a **list** or **challenge** word meaning:
to produce flowers ____________ a violent storm ____________
a type of ship ____________ a wealthy person ____________
a small North American animal ____________
a strong rain-bearing wind of SE Asia ____________

Word Knowledge

Use **list** words to describe the following. (Add to the **list** words if necessary.)
For example: horse = a groomed horse.
eagle ____________ surface ____________
flower ____________ moustache ____________
singer ____________ spoon ____________

WORD history
In Chinese a *tai fung* is a great wind.
Which **list** or **challenge** word do you think has come from the Chinese words *tai fung*?

General Knowledge

1 What am I?
I am a Native American word for a small child. p _ _ _ _ _ _

2 I am a small two-masted vessel with a mainsail and jib. s _ _ _ _ _ _

3 Which **list** word can be used to describe...?
a group of baboons ____________

19

If you are unsure of a word's meaning, look in the Glossary on page 94.
All of the words in this book can be found in the Spelling Reference List beginning on page 86.
Answers are provided at the end of this book.

Classroom Unit 1 ase aste ate as in case waste rate

Your List

fate	rate	slate	inflate	imitate	isolate	educate
case	base	chase	phrase	erase	phase	navigate
haste	waste	taste	paste	baste		illustrate

1 Which **list** words mean…?

a small group of words ______________ cook in fat ______________
to blow up with air ______________ a stage of development ______________
to keep apart ______________ to draw ______________

2 Write words from the **list** in the gaps in these sentences.

We watched the second ______________ of the moon's cycle through a telescope.
The recipe suggested that the chef should ______________ the meat in its own juices.
The glass splintered into a thousand pieces as soon as it hit the ______________ floor.
The clever comedian was able to ______________ the voices of several famous stars.

3 Write the words from the **list** that contain these smaller words.

the opposite of early ______________ ______________ ______________
a rodent ______________ not well ______________

4 Write as **past tense**. For example: base = based.

chase ______________ paste ______________
erase ______________ educate ______________
waste ______________ inflate ______________
imitate ______________ illustrate ______________

Strategy

Look for smaller words.
For example:
phase = has
educate = cat at ate
separate = par rat ate.

Word Building

1 Add the **suffix *ion*** to these **list** or **challenge** words. Remember to drop the ***e*** first.

participate ______________ inflate ______________
imitate ______________ isolate ______________
meditate ______________ eliminate ______________

2 Add words or **suffixes** from Group B to the words in Group A to form new words.

Group A			Group B			
waste	taste	data	ment	base	case	______________
base	tooth	suit	paste	less	paper	______________

Challenge

participate separate eliminate suitcase meditate

Make haste slowly.
(Proverb)

1 All of the **list** words, ending with ***ase*** or ***aste***, are hidden in this Wordsearch. Can you find them?

P	B	A	E	R	A	S	E
P	E	A	C	H	A	S	E
B	H	T	S	P	H	P	S
A	E	R	S	E	A	A	T
S	E	S	A	A	S	S	T
T	T	E	E	S	T	T	A
E	R	S	A	S	E	E	S
W	A	P	H	A	S	E	T
C	T	E	W	A	S	T	E

WORD history

Which of the **list** words do you think has come from the Latin word *insulatus* meaning made into an island?

2 Write one sentence containing: fate and educate.

____

3 Use a dictionary to help you find the meanings of:

imitate ______________________________

phase ______________________________

4 Which **list** words would fit in this Wordframe?

______________ ______________

Word Knowledge

1 Which **challenge** words mean…?

think deeply and seriously ______________ to take part in ______________

to take apart ______________ to get rid of ______________

2 Write **challenge** words in the gaps in these sentences.

We were asked to ______________ in different activities.

Before placing the eggs into the bowl, the cook needed to ______________ the yolks from the whites.

General Knowledge

1 Complete. A sextant is an instrument used to help sailors and pilots ______________.

2 Which **list** or **challenge** words tell what all of the following people do?
professor, tutor, guru, instructor, teacher, pedagogue ______________

3 Which **list** or **challenge** word is a **synonym** for valise? ______________

i_e as in bride

Your List

spice	twice	slice	advice		
outside	collide	guide	decide	provide	divide
strike	spike	capsize			
spire	shire	admire	desire	umpire	require
site	quite	write	polite	invite	
drive	alive	strive	arrive	survive	dive

Look
Say
Cover
Write
Check

1 Circle the correct words in these sentences.
The telescope enabled us to (sight/site) the army's new camp (sight/site).
Part of the ancient (right/write/rite) was to (right/write/rite) the letter Z on the (right/write/rite) arm.

2 Which **list** words mean…?
I am used to flavour food. ______________
I mean to hit or to stop work. ______________
I am an area of local government. ______________
I mean to crash together. ______________
I am the tall pointed part of a building. ______________
I am a referee. ______________

3 Write one interesting sentence containing any three **list** words.
____
____

4 Complete these groups by using a suitable **list** word.
split, cut, slash ______________ referee, judge, adjudicator ______________
salt, cinnamon, pepper ______________ please, thank you, after you ______________

5 Write in alphabetical order: collide, decide, drive, capsize, admire and arrive.
____

Word Building

Add the **suffix *ion*** to the following **list** words.
(The words may need to be changed first.)

divide ______________ collide ______________ decide ______________
admire ______________ invite ______________ provide ______________

Challenge

device	confide	abide	subside	pike	ire	sapphire
perspire	appetite	dynamite	satellite	parasite	deprive	despite

> You may drive out Nature with a pitchfork, yet she'll be constantly running back.
>
> (Horace)

1 How many **list** or **challenge** words can you find in this illustration?

____

2 Complete an **acrostic** for each of the following **list** words. (An **acrostic** is a sentence or poem in which the first letters of each word or line spell a word.)
For example: **Price** = **P**esky **R**ats **I**rritate **C**olossal **E**lephants.

W ________ R ________ I ________ T ________ E ________

S ________ L ________ I ________ C ________ E ________

3 Which **challenge** words mean…?

a fish, a weapon or a type of dive ____________ to sweat ____________

a deep blue gemstone ____________ anger ____________

Word Knowledge

1 Which **list** or **challenge** words do you think come from…?

the Greek word *dunamis* meaning force ____________

the Latin word *satelles* meaning guard ____________

the Greek word *parasitos* meaning one who eats at the table of another ____________

2 Use a dictionary to help you answer the following questions.

What is meant by a trite expression? ____________

What other names can be given for sprites? ____________

General Knowledge

1 What am I?

I am a favourite Australian breakfast or sandwich spread. ____________

2 Would you most likely eat, drink or play chives? ____________

3 What am I?

I am an organism which depends upon another organism for my existence.

____

o_e as in joke

Your List

broke choke poke joke woke smoke spoke stroke
provoke stoke yoke
rove cove drove stove clove grove mangrove
doze froze

1 Write a **list** word in the gaps.

The smugglers waited silently in the quiet ______________ as the ship approached.

Shimmy the dog was able to ______________ lazily on the verandah while the children were at school.

The sheep grazed peacefully in the ______________ of olive trees on the hillside.

2 Which **list** words mean...?

a spice ______________

device used for cooking ______________

past tense of drive ______________

past tense of freeze ______________

to suffocate or stop breathing ______________

prod ______________

to stir up and add fuel ______________

a mudflats tree ______________

3 Use a dictionary to find the meanings of yolk and yoke.
Write each word in a sentence that shows its meaning.

____

____

4 Write in alphabetical order: joke, doze, choke, poke, cove and broke.

____

Word Building

1 Complete.

I will b r__ __ __	I broke	I am b r__ __ __ __ __ __	I have b r__ __ __ __
I will s p__ __ __	I spoke	I am s p__ __ __ __ __ __	I have s p__ __ __ __
I will w__ __ __	I woke	I am w__ __ __ __ __	I have w__ __ __ __

2 Add ***ing*** to the following words. Be careful.

choke ______________ poke ______________ smoke ______________

stroke ______________ stoke ______________ provoke ______________

Challenge

artichoke woven
cloven trove

It is idle to swallow the cow and choke on the tail.

(Proverb)

1 Look carefully at the pairs of words. If they rhyme, place a tick in the box. If they do not rhyme, place a cross in the box.

cove *and* love ☐ rove *and* grove ☐ glove *and* stove ☐

doze *and* does ☐ froze *and* toes ☐ doze *and* goes ☐

2 Which yoke is which yolk?

______________ ______________

WORD history

Cloven is the past tense of cleave, which means to split in two. Can you think of an animal that might have a cloven hoof?

3 Write down the **list** words with:

three **vowels** ______________________________

a double **consonant blend** (for example: ***br cl dr***) at the beginning ______________________________

4 Draw a roving drover *or* someone dozing in a grove.

Word Knowledge

Write **challenge** words in the gaps in these sentences.

A place where treasure can be found in a great quantity is called a treasure ______________.

The expression 'to show the ______________ hoof' means to reveal one's evil side.

The past tense of weave is ______________.

I am a relative of the thistle but I am used as a vegetable. ______________

General Knowledge

1 What am I? I am a tree that grows in tropical estuaries. __ __ __ __ __ __ __ __

2 What am I? I am a solid substance left after heating coal or petrol. __ __ __ __

3 Who am I? I am an ancient Roman god. I am also known as Jupiter. __ __ __ __

une as in dune

Your List

tune	dune	prune	June	fortune
tuneless	tuneful	immune	commune	misfortune

1 Which **list** words mean…?

protected from disease ______________ the sixth month ______________

a sandy hill ______________ musical sounds one after another ______________

great wealth or luck ______________ a group of people living together ______________

bad luck ______________ a dried plum or to trim a plant ______________

2 Write one sentence containing any three **list** words.

____

3 Write any **list** words that are **antonyms** (opposites).

______________ / ______________ ______________ / ______________

4 Write a **list** word in the gap in each of these sentences.

The pirates had buried a ______________ in doubloons and jewels at the foot of the mountain.

The scientists found that insects had become ______________ to their insecticides.

In two months it will be ______________ and the cold winds will arrive.

The busker was able to tap a catchy ______________ with the spoons while standing on his head.

5 Write the **list** words in alphabetical order.

____

____

Word Building

Use the **base word** fortune and the **suffixes** and **prefixes** shown below to form new words.

mis ______________________ ate ______________________

un ______________________ ly ______________________

Make word sums.
For example:
for + tune = fortune
tune + less = tuneless.

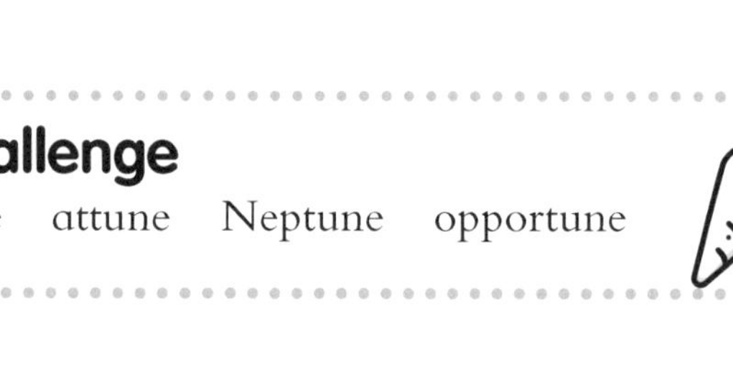

rune attune Neptune opportune

Home Study Unit 4

> Fortune favours the brave.
> (Saying)

1 Use the code A = 26, B = 25, C = 24 etc. to find these **list** words.

7 6 13 22 _ _ _ _   17 6 13 22 _ _ _ _   18 14 14 6 13 22 _ _ _ _ _ _

2 Five of the **list** words can be found by combining the letters in Box A with those in Box B. Write the five words and then write the missing **list** words. (Letters in Box A may be used more than once.)

Box A	Box B
t d f r p j i m	-une

____________ ____________
____________ ____________
____________ ____________
____________ ____________
____________ ____________

Commune comes from the French word *comun* meaning common.
What sort of things do you think a community have in common?

3 Which word?

I am often found near beaches. ____________   I am a month. ____________

I do not have any tune. ____________   To cut (as in gardening). ____________

Word Knowledge

Make new words by adding the **suffix *ity*** to the following words.
Remember to drop the ***e*** before adding the **suffix**.

opportune ____________
immune ____________
commune ____________

Write the new words next to the following definitions.

chance ____________
a group of people living close together ____________
protection from disease ____________

General Knowledge

1 A rune is a character from early Scandinavian and Anglo-Saxon alphabets.
The author of *The Hobbit* and *The Lord of the Rings* developed an alphabet for the elves based upon runes. Who was that author? ____________

2 What is another word for a dried plum? ____________

3 In Roman mythology, who was the god of the sea? ____________

Classroom Unit 5 ee as in deer

Your List

peer	sheer	jeer	sneer	career	volunteer
steer	deer				pioneer
eerie	feel	kneel	steel	reindeer	engineer
reel	peel	wheel	heel	keel	

1 Which **list** word?

I can mean to guide or a male member of the cattle family. ______________

I can mean to look closely or someone of noble birth. ______________

I can mean a spool, to sway or stagger, or a dance. ______________

I am someone who offers to do something without being asked. ________________

I am someone who is first to enter, explore and settle a new region. ________________

I am someone who designs, repairs or makes machinery, bridges etc. ________________

2 Use **list** words to complete these sentences.

The children could each ______________ an ______________ sensation as they approached the haunted house.

The sailor found it impossible to ______________ his boat after the ______________ had been snapped off.

During the race the car's front ______________ had broken from the axle causing the car to ______________ uncontrollably down the hill.

Strategy

Ask which family do words belong to? For example: peel feel reel heel steel and wheel all belong to the same word family.

3 Underline or circle the correct words in these sentences.

Once thousands of wild (deer/dear) roamed the forests of North America.

A (steel/steal) girder was used to support the arch.

Mary was able to (peal/peel) the orange by herself.

Word Building

Add the ending ***ing*** to the following words.

cheer ______________	kneel ______________	peer ______________
sheer ______________	feel ______________	steer ______________

Challenge

mutineer
buccaneer
veneer

> I must go down to the seas again, to the lonely sea and the sky,
> And all I ask is a tall ship and a star to steer her by.
>
> (John Masefield)

1 Match the definitions with **list** or **challenge** words.

so thin you can see through it, or to swerve ______________ strange ______________

the job in which you earn a living, or to move rapidly ______________

to say, or to look in a nasty way ______________

2 Don't get confused! Write the **list** word and its **homophone** (a word that sounds the same as another but is spelt differently) next to the meanings.

a metal ______________ to rob ______________

a grass-eating animal ______________ expensive ______________

back of the foot ______________ to cure ______________

a cylinder or spool ______________ true or actual ______________

to take skin off ______________ to ring out ______________

3 Draw four members of an audience: one cheering, one jeering, one sneering and one kneeling.

Word Knowledge

The word 'veneer' usually means a thin coating of wood or other material. It can, however, be used to describe outwardly pleasant behaviour, disguising what is really underneath. For example: The children's veneer of good manners did not fool their aunt. Write two sentences showing the two meanings of veneer.

____

____

____

____

General Knowledge

1 According to the popular Christmas song, what was the name of the reindeer with a very shiny nose? ______________

2 Who am I? I am another word for pirate. ______________

3 Who am I? I am someone (usually a soldier or sailor) who rebels against authority such as my officers. ______________

ee_e as in geese

Your List

geese	cheese	Greece	fleece	sneeze	freeze	needle	wheeze
squeeze	breeze	sleeve	seethe	beetle	feeble	steeple	

1 Write one sentence containing: fleece, freeze and breeze.

____

____

2 Which **list** words rhyme with…?

peace ______________________

please ______________________

leave ______________ breathe ______________

3 Complete the following sentences using **list** or **challenge** words.

The ____________ of Timmy's jumper had been tied to the church ____________ and now the garment waved gently in the ____________.

It is not unusual to ____________ and ____________ when the winter chill sets in.

4 Which words from the **list** or **challenge** words…?

Strategy

Look at the shape of words. For example:

freeze breeze

cheese.

Word Building

Add *ing* and *ed* to the following words. (Be careful.)

sneeze + ing ____________ sneeze + ed ____________

seethe + ing ____________ seethe + ed ____________

squeeze + ing ____________ squeeze + ed ____________

wheeze + ing ____________ wheeze + ed ____________

Challenge

wheedle

steeplechase

Home Study Unit 6

> With fingers weary and worn,
> With eyelids heavy and red,
> A woman sat, in unwomanly rags,
> Plying her needle and thread—
> (Thomas Hood)

1 Match **list** or **challenge** words with these illustrations.

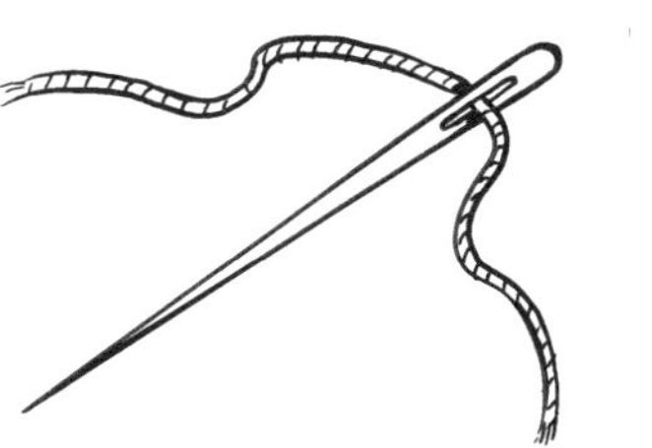

______________ ______________

______________ ______________ ______________

2 Which **list** or **challenge** words mean…?

weak ______________ persuade with flattery ______________

light wind ______________ a race over obstacles ________________

3 *Cryptic Capers*

Which word is an insect containing an insect? ______________

Which word has a male in a dairy product? ______________

Which word suggests running away in a sheep's clothing? ______________

Word Knowledge

Write all of the **list** and **challenge** words that could be associated in any possible way with a cold winter's day. For example: a sheep's warm woollen fleece.

____

____

____

WORD history

The steeplechase was originally a cross-country race in which the village church steeple was in view and served as the goal to be raced to for the competitors.

General Knowledge

1 What is the capital of Greece? ______________

2 At how many degrees Celsius does water freeze? ______________

3 Ganders are the adult males and goslings are the young of what sort of animals? ______________

oo as in scoop

Your List

groom	bloom	droop	scoop	troop	stoop	swoop
cocoon	swoon	monsoon	cartoon	lagoon	croon	baboon
proof	smooth	brood	scooter	shampoo	toadstool	

1 Write the **list** or **challenge** words containing smaller words meaning:

top covering of a house ______________

a chicken's home ______________

meat from a pig ______________

frog-like animal ______________

Strategy

Make short rhymes.
For example: croon to the moon sweep the room with a broom school is cool school is not cool.

2 Write **list antonyms** (opposites) for the following.

rough ______________ straighten ______________

3 Fill the gaps with **list** or **challenge** words.

Each morning a beautiful rose would ______________ under the princess's window.
The resort manager, Mr Gibson, rode his ______________ around the ______________ to see how much damage the heavy ______________ rains had done.
The singer's ______________ made the audience ______________ with delight.
The children eagerly awaited the hatching of the chicken ______________.

4 Which word?

a fungus ______________ an ape ______________ an animation ______________

a caterpillar's home ______________ bend ______________

brush and make tidy ______________

5 Write one sentence containing any three **list** words.

____

____

Word Building

Add ***ing*** and ***ed*** to the following words.

bloom ______________ ______________ swoon ______________ ______________

droop ______________ ______________ swoop ______________ ______________

stoop ______________ ______________ scoop ______________ ______________

Challenge

schooner tycoon
typhoon raccoon

The proof of the pudding is in the eating.
(Proverb)

1 Write all of the words beginning with *s*, from both **lists**, in alphabetical order.

____

2 Which **list** words rhyme with…?
group ________ ________ ________ ________ ________
chewed ________

3 Write a **list** or **challenge** word meaning:
to produce flowers ________ a violent storm ________
a type of ship ________ a wealthy person ________
a small North American animal ________
a strong rain-bearing wind of SE Asia ________

Word Knowledge

Use **list** words to describe the following. (Add to the **list** words if necessary.)
For example: horse = a groomed horse.

eagle ________ surface ________
flower ________ moustache ________
singer ________ spoon ________

WORD history
In Chinese a *tai fung* is a great wind.
Which **list** or **challenge** word do you think has come from the Chinese words *tai fung*?

General Knowledge

1 What am I?
I am a Native American word for a small child. p _ _ _ _ _ _ _

2 I am a small two-masted vessel with a mainsail and jib. s _ _ _ _ _ _ _

3 Which **list** word can be used to describe…?
a group of baboons ________

8 ou as in round

Your List

round	hound	sound	ground	surround	found	mound	bound
count	amount	account	couch	pouch	south	mouth	stout
bout	foul	aloud	bounce	pounce	pound	crouch	fountain
doubt	lounge	bough	arouse	sour	mountain		

1 Read the paragraph below and then write out all of the **list** or **challenge** words contained in it. (Or words formed from **list** or **challenge** words.)

> As we travelled along the south boundary of the mountain reserve, we found a great deal of evidence to suggest, without doubt, that the hound had visited us around dawn. Close to a low-hanging tree bough we observed tracks on the ground at the mouth of Thompson's Cave. Taking cover behind a mound of coarse sandstone, we waited quietly. Before long we heard a sound that made even our stout hearts pound. A shrill howl pierced the air and within seconds one hound after another began to bound towards us from the cave and soon we were surrounded by a pack of crouching, foul-breathed wild dogs ready to pounce.

____
____
____
____
____
____
____
____
____
____
____
____

2 Which **list** or **challenge** words are **antonyms** (opposites) for the following?

lost ______________ real ______________ square ______________

sweet ______________ skinny ______________ silently ______________

Look
Say
Cover
Write
Check

3 Which **list** or **challenge** words are **synonyms** for the following words?

sofa ______________ rebound ______________

limb ______________ pile ______________

Word Building

Match the word parts to form new words.

south	account		wards	count	
dis	under	+	about	room	
round	lounge		ant	ful	
doubt			ground	dog	

______________ ______________
______________ ______________
______________ ______________
______________ ______________

Challenge

boundary announce
council foundation
counterfeit encounter

Home Study Unit 8

> Empty vessels make the most sound.
>
> (Proverb)

1 In this Wordsearch all of the **list** words that end with a **consonant blend** are hidden. For example: grou<u>nd</u>. Can you find them all?

```
G O B O U G H C H C O U C H
A R G O B A T R N O D O U U
C U N R U M O O U O U D O N
C O U C O O W U O D I N M D
O D C T T U N C A B H U D S
U N O N U N N H U T H O F O
N U U O H T F D U T T M O U
T O T C O U T O D O U B T N
C F U R O U S T H E O O U D
R O U N D B O U N D M S N O
P O U N D S U R R O U N D O
```

2 Draw a cat about to pounce upon a hound from a bough.

Word Knowledge

Select any two **challenge** words. Find the definition of each. Then write them in sentences that show their meanings.

____

____

General Knowledge

1 How many fouls can an Olympic basketball player commit before being asked to leave the court? ____________

2 What do the following have in common?
Kilimanjaro, Everest, Mont Blanc, Kosciuszko, Fuji ____________________

3 Which **list** word could be used before each of these to form place names?
Australia, Pole, -port, Korea, -hampton, Africa ____________

ou as in double

Your List

double	country	couple	rough	touch	cousin	young
trouble	courage	encourage	tough	flourish	nourish	

1 Write the list words in alphabetical order.

___

___

___

___

2 Write the following **list** words in sentences to show their meanings. If necessary use a dictionary to help you.

double ___

___

couple ___

___

cousin ___

___

courage ___

___

encourage ___

___

3 Match with meanings:

flourish	to feed
doubloon	a young person
youngster	to grow strongly
nourish	an old Spanish coin often stolen by pirates

Strategy

Look for smaller words.
For example:
flourish = our flour
encourage = courage rage age.

Word Building

Someone who is full of courage is said to be c o u r a g e __ __ __.

Someone who causes trouble is said to be a t r o u b l e __ __ __ __ __.

Someone who is young is a y o u n g __ __ __ __.

Someone who is a rough and rowdy person is a r o u g h __ __ __ __.

Challenge

courageous youngster troublemaker doubloon roughneck

> Never trouble trouble till trouble troubles you.
> (Proverb)

1 Match the meanings with **list** words.

bravery ______________ feel ______________

difficulty ______________ son or daughter of aunt or uncle ______________

to cheer on ______________ land beyond towns and cities ______________

twice as much ______________ not easily cut, broken or worn out ______________

2 Which **list** words would fit into these Wordframes?

3 Which **list** or **challenge** words contain smaller words that mean…?

anger ______________ ______________ ______________

ground grain ______________ wickedness ______________

Word Knowledge

A cousin is a relative. How many other types of relatives can you list?

____

____

____

WORD history

Cor is a Latin word meaning heart.

Coeur is a French word meaning heart.

Which **list** or **challenge** words do you think have come from these words, and what have they to do with the heart?

General Knowledge

1 Name the countries or areas from which these well-known dishes have come.

kebabs ______________ lasagne ______________ pita bread ______________

goulash ______________ souvlaki ______________ satay ______________

tacos ______________ tandoori ______________ quiche ______________

sushi ______________ pizza ______________ chow mein ______________

2 Which **list** word would best match the awarding of the Victoria Cross? ______________

3 Which **list** or **challenge** word would best be used in describing what the Braille system is? ______________

Classroom Unit 10 ow as in power

Your List

power	tower	cower	shower	flower	glower	however	bowel
towel	vowel	dowel	coward	powder	drowsy	allow	trowel

Strategy

Look for smaller words.
For example:
coward = cow war ward
glower = glow low lower.

1 Write the **list** words in alphabetical order.

____
____
____
____

2 Circle the correct word in these sentences.

After it was sifted, the salt was added to the (flower/flour) before the cooking began.

Because they had played their music (aloud/allowed), the children were not (aloud/allowed) to leave their room.

Spring becomes an exciting time as each (flower/flour) bursts into new life.

3 Circle the vowels in these **list** and **challenge** words.

cauliflower   powder   cowardice   however

4 Which **list** words would you most likely associate with the following?

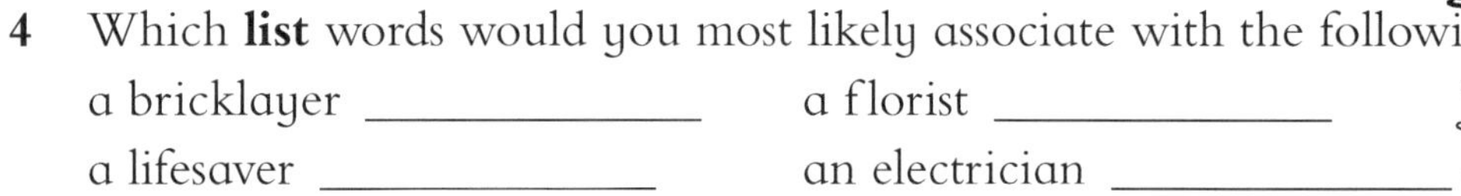

a bricklayer ______________ a florist ______________

a lifesaver ______________ an electrician ______________

a carpenter ______________ a doctor ______________

5 Which **list** or **challenge** words mean…?

sleepy ______________ to draw away from in fear ______________

to stare angrily ______________ someone who acts badly through fear ______________

money traditionally brought by a woman to her marriage ______________

Word Building

Add **suffixes** from the list on the right to form new words.

power		ance	______________	______________
coward		less	______________	______________
allow	+	ly	______________	______________
how		ful		
		ever		
		ice		

Challenge

dowry   cowardice   cauliflower   bower

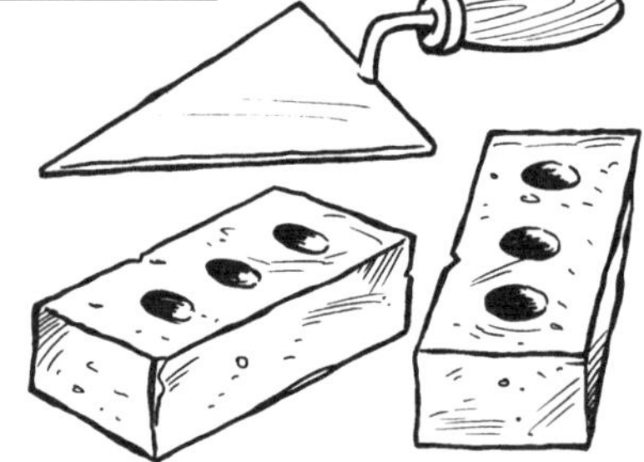

Home Study Unit 10

> Knowledge itself is power.
> (Francis Bacon)

1 Use the **list** or **challenge** words to help you complete this Crossword.

Across
1 draw away in fear
5 ability to do something
6 sleepy

Down
1 one who is afraid
2 gift at marriage
3 bricklayer's tool
4 give permission

2 Write one interesting sentence containing any three **list** or **challenge** words.

____

____

3 Which **list** words best suit the following?

beach, tea, bath ____________ sand, brick, mortar ____________

rose, tulip, carnation ____________ Eiffel, Eureka, Centrepoint ____________

Word Knowledge

Can you find the names of fifteen flowers that can also be used as people's names?

____

____

____

____

____

WORD history

The words 'coward' and 'cowardice' come from the Latin word *caudra*, which means tail. When an animal is frightened it puts its tail between its legs. So a coward has come to be compared with a frightened animal.

General Knowledge

1 In which European capital city does the Tower Bridge cross the Thames? ____________

2 Write down the five vowels. __ __ __ __ __

3 The male Satin Bower bird collects objects of a certain colour to place in his *bower* to attract females. What colour do you think this would be? ____________

ow as in shadow

Your List

tomorrow	swallow	willow	sorrow	shallow	fellow	billow
sparrow	narrow	marrow	wheelbarrow	burrow	furrow	borrow
bellow	hollow	elbow	shadow	meadow	window	

1 Write all of the double-*r* words in alphabetical order.

____

____

Strategy

Put words into families.
For example:
barrow marrow narrow
hollow follow fellow bellow
yellow billow willow pillow.

2 Which words?

sadness ______________ a vegetable ______________
thin ______________ a tree ______________
empty ______________ shout ______________

3 Which **list** words best match with the following?

______________ sill ______________ boxing ______________ grease

4 Use a dictionary to help you write the definitions of these words.

harrow ______________________________
furrow ______________________________
wallow ______________________________
sallow ______________________________
billow ______________________________
burrow ______________________________

Word Building

Add *ing* to the following words and then write each in a sentence.

billow ______________ ______________________________

____

bellow ______________ ______________________________

____

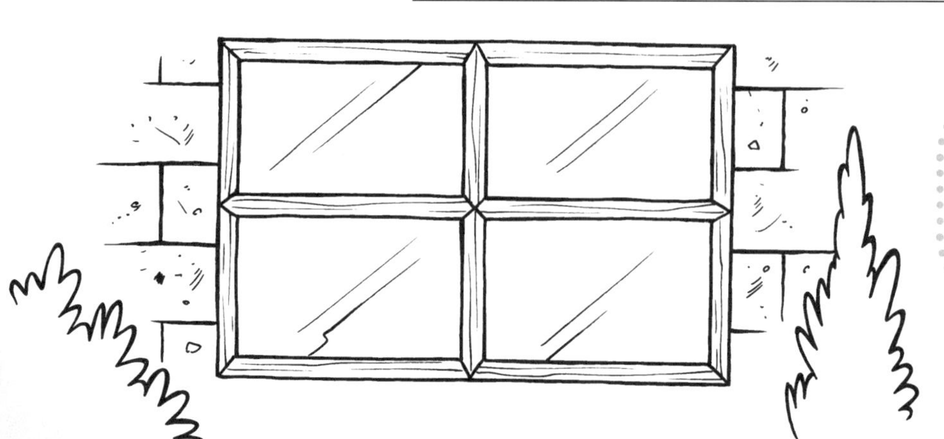

Challenge

harrow
wallow
sallow

Home Study Unit 11

He that goes a-borrowing,
goes a-sorrowing.
(Proverb)

1 Find 13 **list** words hidden in this Wordsearch.

F	W	W	B	U	R	R	O	W
E	E	S	W	A	L	L	O	W
L	O	L	F	U	R	R	O	W
L	A	W	B	O	R	R	O	W
O	W	O	H	O	L	L	O	W
W	I	N	D	O	W	R	A	W
O	L	A	A	R	R	O	W	B
W	L	R	W	A	Y	L	O	B
R	O	R	M	E	A	D	O	W
A	W	O	L	L	E	Y	R	O
W	O	W	B	I	L	L	O	W

2 Which **list** words are **antonyms** for these words?

wide ________________ deep ________________

lend ________________ solid ________________

3 Draw a fellow on a narrow window ledge, shooting an arrow at a billowing cloud.

Word Knowledge

Match the **challenge** words with these definitions.

A heavy frame with iron teeth used to break clods of earth. ____________________

A sickly yellow colour, usually of skin. ____________________

Roll about in mud, sand or water. ____________________

General Knowledge

1 Where, in the human body, would you find the humerus? ________________

2 Name a creature that enjoys wallowing. ________________

3 Name the soft fatty substance in the middle of bones. ________________

oa as in roar

Your List

oar	roar	boar	soar	board	hoard	hoarse
aboard	cupboard	cardboard		uproar	coarse	skateboard

1 Write the **list** or **challenge** words that contain smaller words with the following meanings.

a vehicle ______________ a drinking vessel ______________

2 Find the **list** or **challenge** words that mean:

a long paddle ______________ loud disturbance ______________
male pig ______________ loud deep sound ______________
grey or white with age ______________ a storage place ______________

3 Which word? Circle the correct word in the brackets.

The cowboy became (hoarse/horse) calling for his (hoarse/horse).

All of the golfers complained that the sand on the golf (coarse/course) was too (coarse/course).

The wild (boar/bore) used its tusks to (boar/bore) a hole into the fence.

Once Harry's (soar/sore) leg had healed he was able to (soar/sore) to new heights in his hang glider.

The children quickly became (board/bored) with the work displayed upon the (board/bored).

A (hoard/horde) of bandits had arrived to (hoard/horde) the treasure for themselves.

Word Building

A **compound word** is one word made from two words. For example: bed + room = bedroom. Write the four **compound words** from the **list**.
(Note: 'a' in aboard is a **prefix** rather than a word.)

____

Strategy

All of the **list** words contain the smaller word 'oar'.

Challenge

hoary

Home Study Unit 12

> Water, water, everywhere,
> And all the boards did shrink;
> (Samuel T. Coleridge)

1 Fill in the missing letters to make **list** or **challenge** words.

s _ _ r　　h o _ _ s e　　_ _ a _ y　　c _ _ b _ _ r d

_ _ _ o a r　　b _ a _ d　　c _ _ _ _ e　　b _ _ _

2 Write in alphabetical order, all the **list** words containing *board*.

WORD history

The decks of sailing ships were once made of wooden boards. To be *aboard* a ship meant to be on deck.

3 Which **list** words rhyme with force?

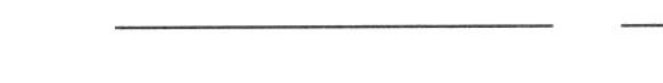

4 Which **list** words?

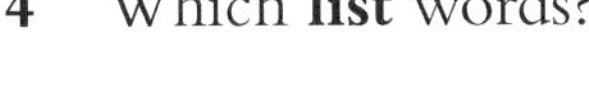

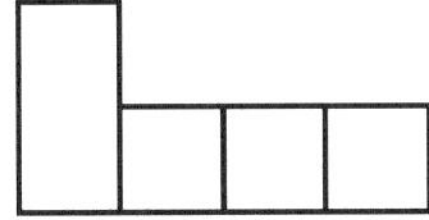

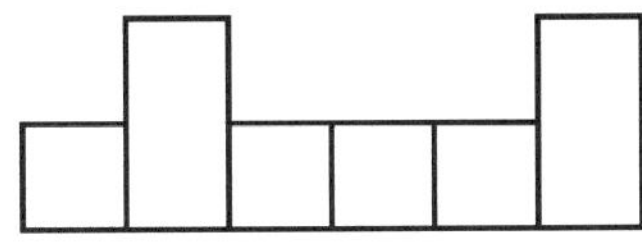

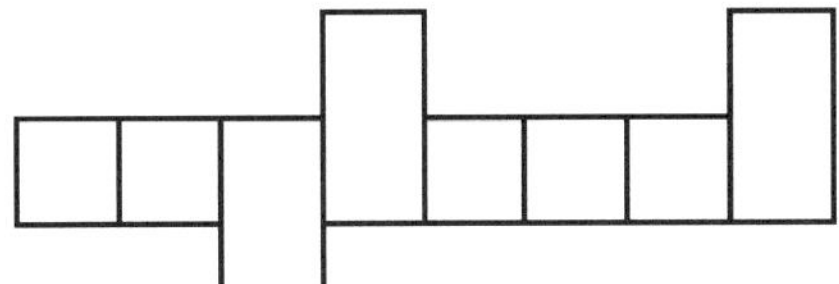

Word Knowledge

An **adverb** is a word that tells us more about another word (that is a verb).

For example: We can say 'the children walked to the shop' or 'the children walked happily to the shop'. (*Happily* is an **adverb** because it tells how the children walked.)

Change coarse and hoarse to **adverbs** by adding ***ly***.

coarse + ly = ______________　　hoarse + ly = ______________

Write each new word in a sentence.

____

____

General Knowledge

1 Match the following animals with their mates.

boar	nanny-goat
bull	ewe
ram	doe
buck	cow
stallion	sow
billy-goat	mare

2 What is the name given to the long paddle used to row a boat? ______________

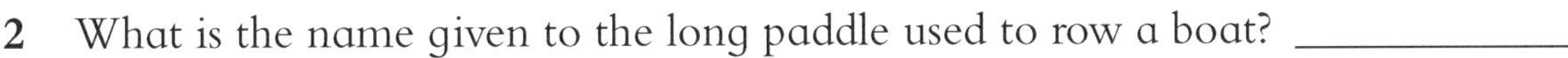

3 Which **list** or **challenge** word would be a good adjective to describe Gandalf the old wizard from J.R.R. Tolkien's *The Hobbit* and *The Lord of the Rings*? ______________

Classroom Unit 13 ai as in aid

Your List

aid	laid	maid	paid	raid	afraid	mermaid
raise	waist	maize	daisy	praise	bait	gait
aim	claim	maim	raisin	straight	strait	

1 Which **list** words fit into these Wordframes?

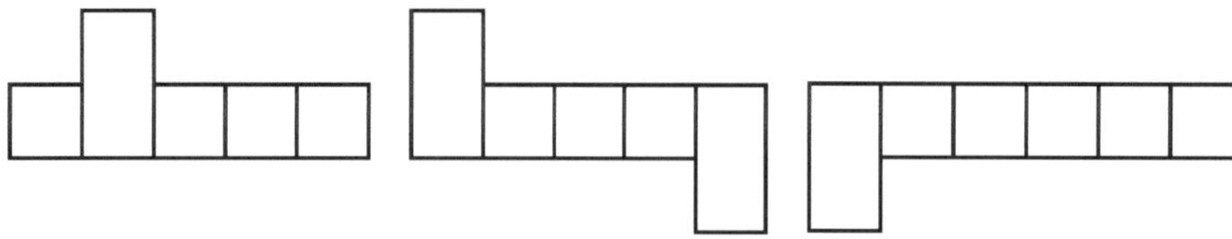

Strategy

Use memory triggers. For example:
Don't aim to maim.
M comes to the aid of a maid.

2 Which **list** or **challenge** words are disguised in these **acrostics**?

Many Armies Invaded Mesopotamia ______________

Rabbits Ate In Silent Excitement ______________

Little Ants Irritated Danny ______________

Write your own **acrostic** sentence using these **list** words.

b ____________ a ____________ i ____________ t ____________

w ____________ a ____________ i ____________ s ____________ t ____________

c ____________ l ____________ a ____________ i ____________ m ____________

3 Which **list** words are **homonyms** for these words?

rays ______________ strait ______________

waste ______________ straight ______________

4 Use a dictionary to help you define these **challenge** words.

mayonnaise ____

renaissance ____

exclaim ____

Word Building

Join the word parts to form new words.

mis	praise	+	claim	laid	______________ ______________ ______________
re	aim		less	worthy	______________ ______________

Challenge

bridesmaid mayonnaise exclaim renaissance

Self-praise is no recommendation.
(Proverb)

1 Write the missing letters.
m a __ __ __ m __ __ m __ a i __ t m __ __ m __ __ d

2 Which words?
a flower __________ to lift __________ a servant __________
to injure the body __________ a sea nymph __________

3 Match the meanings with the following **homophones**.

body part between ribs and hips	waste
throw away needlessly	maid
cereal plant	waist
female servant	maize
puzzling pathways	made
produced	maze

4 Write the **list** or **challenge** words that are foods.

____

5 Which words from the **list** come from…?
pray __________ lie __________
pay __________

WORD history

In Old English the word used for sea or lake was *mere*. Which of the **list** or **challenge** words means woman of the sea?

Word Knowledge

Choose a suitable **list** or **challenge** word for each of the following groups?

Help! Go away! Well done! __________

rose, carnation, pansy __________

walk, pace, stride __________

General Knowledge

1 Who wrote the story 'The Little Mermaid' (or 'The Little Sea Maiden')? __________

2 The period, in art history, from 1400 to 1600 is called the Renaissance period. During this period there were many famous artists. Name the famous Renaissance artist who painted the 'Mona Lisa'?
L __________ da V __________

3 Which of these is not an ingredient of mayonnaise?
eggs, raisins, oil, lemon juice/vinegar __________

Classroom Unit 14 ea as in heap

Your List

heap	reap	cheap	weary	wreath	sheath	feature
easy	eager	reason	season	treason	sheaf	creature
easel	weasel	eagle	measles	treacle	cheat	

1 Write one interesting sentence containing any three **list** words.

____

____

2 Use a dictionary to find and write the definitions of:

sheaf ____________________________________

wreath ____________________________________

sheath ____________________________________

3 Match the following occupations with the best **list** or **challenge** words.

farmer	knead
traitor	sheaf
chef	creature
biologist	treason
artist	eagle
ornithologist	easel

Look for smaller words.
For example:
treason = reason son on
weary = wear ear.

Word Building

To change weary and easy to **adverbs** (words that help to describe a verb), change ***y*** to ***i*** and then add ***ly***. Change both words to **adverbs** and then write each in a sentence.

weary ____________________________________

____

easy ____________________________________

____

Challenge

knead heathen meagre cleat

It is easy to be wise after the event.
(Proverb)

1 Draw a creature with the following features: an eagle-like nose, weasel-like ears, skin with measles and eager eyes.

2 Use the **list** and **challenge** words to complete this Crossword.

1 pagan
2 bird
3 pile
4 not hard
5 sticky liquid
6 add flavour

3 Which **list** or **challenge** words?

I begin with a silent letter. ______________ ______________

I end with a **vowel**. ______________ ______________ ______________ ______________ ______________

4 Which **list** or **challenge** words contain smaller words that mean…?

a listening organ ______________ the ocean ______________

to consume food ______________ ______________ ______________ ______________ ______________ ______________ ______________

Word Knowledge

Which word? Circle the correct word.

The farmer loaded the (sheaf/sheath) of hay onto the truck.

The fisherman kept the sharp knife in a leather (sheaf/sheath).

To make sure the bread rises properly you must (knead/need) it for at least ten minutes.

You (knead/need) to build your muscles up if you are to become stronger.

General Knowledge

1 Write the names of the four seasons.

______________ ______________ ______________ ______________

2 In which country might you find Rotorua, Mt Cook, Kiwis, the All Blacks and Silver Ferns?

____

3 Complete: Bering ______________, ______________ of Japan, Black ______________, Caspian ______________, South China ______________, Timor ______________, Mediterranean ______________.

Classroom Unit 15 ea as in steak

Your List

steak	great	break	pleasant	peasant	heather	breakthrough
deaf	death	breath	feather	weather	leather	
threat	sweat	weapon	jealous	heavy	heaven	

1 Write the **list** words that rhyme with fake, in alphabetical order.

____

2 **Homophones** are words that sound the same but are spelt differently. For example: steak and stake. Match these **list** words and their **homophones** with the following meanings:

great/grate	a frame of metal ____________	large ____________
steak/stake	thick slice of meat ____________	stick with pointed end ____________
weather/whether	state of the atmosphere ____________	which of the two ____________
break/brake	something to slow or to stop ____________	divide into pieces ____________

3 Write **list** words that are **synonyms** (words with similar meanings) for:

perspiration ____________ plume ____________ envious ____________

delightful ____________ development ____________ weighty ____________

4 Which **list** words best fit into these sentences?

We waited patiently for a ____________ forecast before setting off on our picnic.

The frightened children held their ____________ as the stranger approached.

From the crown of the princess's hat rose a single blue ____________.

A single ____________ strap held the battered old suitcase together.

5 Which **list** word can be a girl's name or a type of shrub? ________________

Word Building

1 Add the word break to form new words. The clues may help.

break __ __ __ __ (first meal) break __ __ __ __ __ __ __ (new development)

break __ __ __ __ (at a dangerous speed) break __ __ __ __ (collapse or failure)

2 Add ***ly*** to the following words and then write each new word in a sentence.

pleasant ______________________________________

heaven ______________________________________

death ______________________________________

Challenge

pheasant treachery treacherous breaststroke

Home Study Unit 15

> There is really no such thing as bad weather, only different kinds of good weather.
>
> (John Ruskin)

1 Complete this Wordsearch using the following **list** words.

```
H B R E A K F A S T L
E H A D B E R A W H E
A C E E A R E C E D A
V F E A T H E R A E T
E A E F V M E A T A H
N R E A T E A E T T E
B E A S T E A K H H R
```

breakfast
heaven
breath
leather
deaf
steak
death
sweat
feather

WORD history

The Old French word *tricher* means cheat. Which **list** or **challenge** words do you think come from the word *tricher*?

2 Decode the following words using this number code: A = 2, B = 4, C = 6, D = 8, etc.

46 10 2 40 16 10 36 ______________ 16 10 2 44 10 28 ______________

4 36 10 2 22 ______________ 40 16 36 10 2 40 ______________

3 Which **list** words are disguised in these **acrostics**?

Some tigers eat appetising kernels. ________________

Silently we entered another tunnel. ________________

Happy echidnas always volunteer each November. ______________

4 Which **list** words do the following **base words** belong to?

breathe ______________ please ______________ die ______________

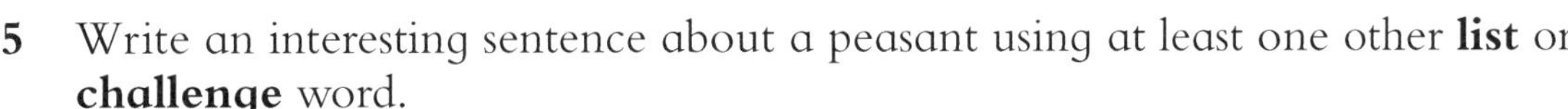

5 Write an interesting sentence about a peasant using at least one other **list** or **challenge** word.

____

Word Knowledge

Circle the best answer.

Which colour is usually associated with jealousy?	red green blue
Who might commit treachery?	tracker traitor trainer
Which house is a peasant likely to live in?	mansion palace hut
Who is more likely to achieve a breakthrough?	scientist signwriter sentry
Who is likely to be most pleasant in manner?	troll ogre fairy

General Knowledge

1 Of which country was Catherine the Great the ruler? ________________

2 In which country is the Great Wall ? ______________________

3 Who wrote the novel *Great Expectations*? ____________________________

Classroom Unit 16 au as in caught

Your List

caught	naughty	daughter	haughty	saucer	caution	fault	assault
taught	slaughter	onslaught	sauce	applaud	vault	dinosaur	somersault

1 Write a suitable **list** word in the gaps in the following sentences.

The concert pianist was accompanied on his tour by his son and his ______________.

After the orchestra had completed its first item of the concert, the audience began to ______________ loudly.

All of the children had been ______________ to wait patiently in line.

After making one hundred and one runs, the batter was ______________ and bowled by his brother.

Too much ______________ on your meat will spoil the taste.

'I'm sorry but it was my ______________ that the paint spilt everywhere,' confessed Freddy.

Strategy

Look at the shape of the word.
For example: daughter.

2 Which **list** words mean the same as these…?

arrogant ______________ mischievous ______________

jump ______________ kill ______________

attack ______________ care ______________

3 Which **list** or **challenge** words would you associate with the following groups?

Tyrannosaurus Rex, Stegosaurus, Diplodocus ______________

half twist, pike, balance ______________

plate, cup, dish ______________

Word Building

To change the following words to **adverbs** (words that help to describe a verb) change ***y*** to ***i*** then add ***ly***.

naughty becomes n a u g h t __ __ __ haughty becomes h a u g h t __ __ __

Use a dictionary to help you define these words. Write each one in a sentence.

____

____

____

____

Challenge

gauze
audio
precaution
authentic
audition
auburn
bauxite

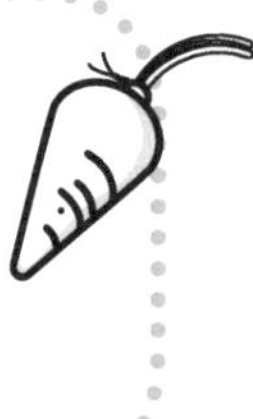

A fault confessed is half redressed.
(Proverb)

1 Use a dictionary to help you define the following words.

authentic ______
auburn ______
auditorium ______
bauxite ______
gauze ______
auger ______
haughty ______

2 Which **list** words?

_ _ a u g _ _ e r   s _ _ _ e r   n _ _ _ _ t y

3 Write the following words in alphabetical order: slaughter, saucer, somersault and sauce.

______

Word Knowledge

The **prefix** ***audio*** means to hear. Match the following audio words with their meanings.

audiometer	one who has great interest in sound reproduction
audiology	a sound tape recording
audiovisual	the scientific study of hearing
audiotape	an instrument for measuring hearing
audiophile	both heard and seen

General Knowledge

1 List the names of ten dinosaurs.

______

______

2 What abbreviation can be used to describe a flying saucer? ______

3 What am I? I am mined to make aluminium. ______

Classroom Unit 17 ei as in reign

Your List

eight	eighty	eighteen	reign	rein	reindeer
eighth	sleigh	neigh	neighbour	vein	
freight	foreign	veil	weigh	weight	leisure

1 Which **list** or **challenge** words?
I am the number before 19. ______________
I am the number after seventy-nine. ______________
In the race I came after the seventh runner. I came ______________.
I am the result of four multiplied by two. ______________

2 Which **list** words rhyme with hay? ______________ ______________ ______________

3 Which **list** words rhyme with ate? ______________ ______________ ______________

4 Which **list** words rhyme with cane? ______________ ______________ ______________

5 Circle or underline the correct word in the brackets.
The monarch kept a very tight (reign/rein) on his subjects during his long (reign/rein).
Blood flows through your (vain/vein) to your heart.
The sailors battled in (vain/vein) to save their sinking ship.
We caught sight of the beautiful (vale/veil) as the (vale veil) of mist rose slowly.
The patients were asked to (wait/weight) quietly while each had their (wait/weight) measured on the hospital scales.
For lunch the children (ate/eight) (ate/eight) slices each.

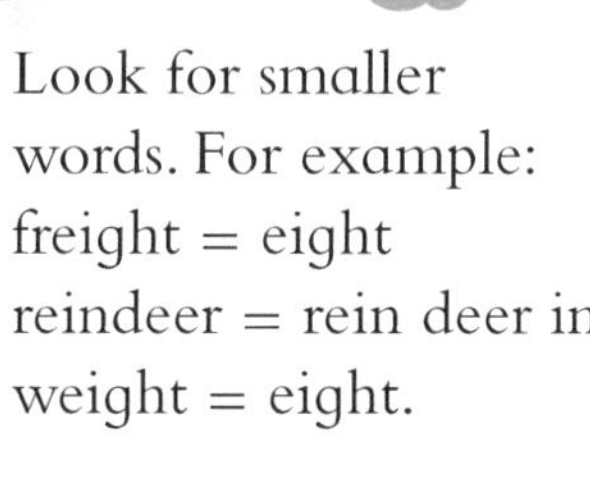

Strategy

Look for smaller words. For example:
freight = eight
reindeer = rein deer in
weight = eight.

Word Building

1 Which **list** word is a **compound word**? ______________

2 Add the **suffixes** or **prefixes** shown in brackets to each word and then match with their meanings.

weight (less) ________________	weighing too much
neighbour (hood) ________________	at an easy pace
(over) weight ________________	having no weight
leisure (ly) ________________	area in which you live

Challenge

heifer

When your neighbour's wall is on fire, it becomes your business.
(Horace)

1 Write the following words in alphabetical order: eight, eighty, eighteen and eighth.

____

2 Write the following words in numerical order: eight, eighty and eighteen.

____

3 Match the following definitions with **list** or **challenge** words.
a young cow that has not calved ____________ a time free from work ____________

4 Draw a sleigh being pulled by a reindeer *or* eight reigning kings or queens.

Word Knowledge

Which **list** or **challenge** words would best fit into these groups?

necktie, scarf, yashmak ____________ calf, steer, bullock ____________

bridle, harness, bit ____________ toboggan, luge, sled ____________

General Knowledge

1 The circulatory system deals with the circulation of the blood. Find out what each of the following parts of the circulatory system does.

vein ______________________________

artery ______________________________

aorta ______________________________

ventricle ______________________________

2 Which **list** or **challenge** words best match the following?

king and queen ____________ octagon ____________

truck ____________ octogenarian ____________

3 Which **list** word is likely to pull or drag another **list** word? ____________

Classroom Unit 18 ie as in believe

Your List

believe	achieve	grieve	retrieve	relieve		
brief	grief	chief	thief	belief	relief	handkerchief
pier	pierce	fierce	field	shield	wield	yield
fiend	shriek	siege	priest	diesel	niece	piece

1 Write all of the **list** words that begin with *f* in alphabetical order.

____

2 Use a dictionary to help you to write definitions for the following words.

retrieve ______________________________

yield ______________________________

siege ______________________________

fiend ______________________________

grieve ______________________________

wield ______________________________

3 Write one interesting sentence containing any three **list** words.

____

4 Piece and peace are **homophones**. Write each word in a sentence to show the difference in meanings of the two words.

____

____

____

____

These list words follow the rule 'i before e'.

5 Match the following definitions with **list** or **challenge** words.

I perform religious ceremonies. ______________

I am a loud, piercing scream. ______________

I mean to get or bring back. ______________

I am a type of fuel. ______________

I am important in a hospital. ______________

I am used for protection. ______________

Word Building

Add the **suffix** or **prefix** shown in brackets to form new words.

achieve + (ment) = ______________

(de) + brief = ______________

grieve + (ance) = ______________

chief + (tain) = ______________

fiend + (ish) = ______________

(dis) + belief = ______________

Challenge

hygiene reprieve

> Do you believe in fairies…?
> If you believe, clap your hands!
> (J. M. Barrie)

1 Use a suitable **list** word to fill the gaps in the following sentences.

The silent ______________ crept slowly towards the jewels.

Danny had trained his dog to ______________ a stick from even the deepest water.

The warrior had been fortunate that not one spear had been able to ______________ his metal ______________.

The guinea pigs were alarmed by a ______________ ______________ as the eagle swooped towards them.

2 Make the following words **plurals** (more than one).

belief ______________ niece ______________ thief ______________

handkerchief ______________ chief ______________ priest ______________

3 Draw a fiendish thief with a handkerchief covering his face.

Word Knowledge

Relieve (**verb**) and relief (**noun**) belong as a pair. Write two other similar pairs from the **list**. Write whether each word is a **verb** (something that can be done) or a **noun** (the name of something).

Verb	**Noun**
______________	______________
______________	______________

General Knowledge

1 A niece is a type of relative. What sort of relatives are the following?

your male parent ______________

son of your brother or sister ______________

the woman who gave birth to you ______________

sister of your father or mother ______________

your mother's mother ______________

the man married to your sister ______________

brother of your father or mother ______________

child of your uncle or aunt ______________

2 What type of transport is likely to make use of a pier? ______________

3 Was a druid a Celtic… shield, siege, priest or chief? ______________

WORD history

In 1892 Dr Rudolf Diesel invented an engine in which compressed air ignites fuel rather than a spark (as in a petrol engine).

Today diesel engines are commonly used in ships, railway locomotives, for electricity generation and for many road vehicles such as trucks and four-wheel-drive cars.

19 ui ue as in juice argue

Your List

bruise	cruise	juice	fruit	suit	recruit	suitable	
clue	blue	cue	due	glue	flue	true	rue
value	issue	rescue	tissue	argue	queue	avenue	barbecue
duel	fuel	cruel	pursue	statue	continue	revenue	

1 Which **list** words are **homophones** (words that sound the same but are spelt differently) for…?

blew ________________ queue ________________ dew ________________

flew ________________ brews ________________ crews ________________

2 Write these **list homophones** in sentences to show their meanings.

bruise ________________

cue ________________

queue ________________

flue ________________

3 Which word?

You might use me if you have a cold. ________________

I can be used to mend a broken toy. ________________

You might eat me. ________________

You might drink me. ________________

4 Write in alphabetical order: clue, blue, fruit, rescue, flue and fuel.

____

5 Write dictionary definitions for:

issue ________________

subdue ________________

Strategy

Make word families.
For example:
fruit suit,
bruise cruise,
duel fuel cruel.

Word Building

Add the **suffix** or **prefix** shown to form new words.

argue + ment (careful) ________________

suit + able ________________

un + suit + able ________________

value + able (careful) ________________

virtue + ous (careful) ________________

recruit + ment ________________

Challenge

accrue subdue venue virtue

Home Study Unit 19

He that would eat the fruit must climb the tree.
(Proverb)

1 Use **list** or **challenge** words to complete this Crossword.

Across
1 outside meal
4 energy supply
5 to be convenient
8 save
9 sticky stuff!
10 billiard stick

Down
1 body mark
2 regret
3 hint
6 real
7 liquid

2 Which **list** or **challenge** words?

tree lined road ________________
coast along ________________
worth ________________
newly joined member ________________
quarrel ________________
special contest ________________

3 Which **challenge** words mean...?

accumulate ________________
scene of an event ________________

Word Knowledge

Add *ing* to the following words. The *e* must be dropped first.

issue ________________ value ________________ subdue ________________
argue ________________ rescue ________________

General Knowledge

1 Which of the following are not fruits?
paw paw, guava, artichoke, zucchini, mango
____________ ____________

2 What kind of drink is made from fermented juice of grapes? ____________

3 Name any type of fossil fuel. ____________

WORD history

Barbecue comes from a Spanish word, *barbacoa*. In the West Indies the same word *barbacoa* was used to describe either a wooden bed or a large cooking iron upon which a whole animal could be roasted.

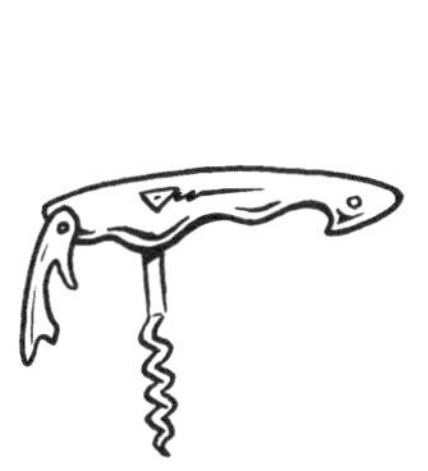

The magic e and vowel sounds

Classroom Review 1

Your List

taste	fortune	rough	grain	entertain				
skate	sneer	enough	disease	believe	white	spool	pillow	autumn
dice	cheese	growl	meant	suitable	awoke	around	tomorrow	August

1 Write the **list** words that contain smaller words that mean:

a stronghold ______________ frozen water ______________

set of clothes ______________ ocean ______________

water from the sky ______________ puddle of water ______________

2 Write one interesting sentence containing any three **list** words.

____

____

3 Use a dictionary to help you write the meanings of these words.

spool ____

sneer ____

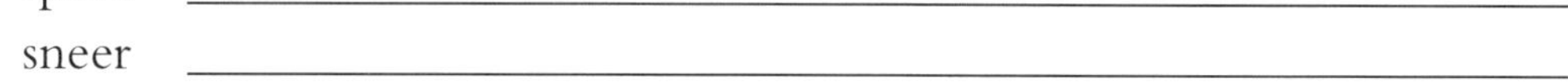

Strategy

Look
Say
Cover
Write
Check

4 Which **list** words?

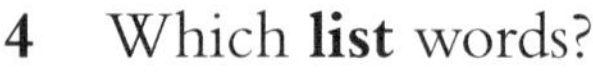

__ n __ __ g h   s __ __ t __ __ __ __   __ __ m __ __ __ __ w

5 Which **list** words rhyme with the following…?

bent ______________ height ______________ cuff ______________

soak ______________ wait ______________ hear ______________

6 Match the definitions with the **list** words shown.

a tiny particle	autumn
a season	dice
the day after today	disease
small game cubes	grain
a dairy product	tomorrow
an illness	cheese

Word Building

Add the ending shown for each word (be careful) and then write the new word in a sentence.

believe + (able) ____

taste + (ful) ____

fortune + (ate) ____

entertain + (ment) ____

Challenge

statuesque theatre nuisance

Home Study Review

Never put off till tomorrow what you can do today.
(Proverb)

Classroom Review 1

1 Which **list** words fit into these Wordframes?

2 Which **list** words?
I begin with a capital letter. ________
I contain a doubled **consonant**. ________ ________
I begin with a **vowel**. ________ ________ ________
________ ________ ________
I contain a doubled **vowel**. ________ ________ ________

3 Draw a sneering cheese, a growling dice and a skating pillow.

4 Which **list** words match the following…?

cotton, yarn ________ chicken pox, measles ________
summer, winter ________ Snakes and Ladders, Monopoly ________
today, yesterday ________ June, December ________

5 Which **list** words are **antonyms** (opposites) for the following…?

black ________ smooth ________
bore ________ spring ________

Word Knowledge

Use the three **challenge** words in one interesting sentence.

____

____

General Knowledge

1 Which season do North Americans call Fall? ________

2 What do the following have in common?
Camembert, Edam, Gouda, Cheddar ________

3 What do we call the seeds produced by wheat, oats and barley? ________

sc spl sch squ as in scar split scheme squid

Your List

scatter	scarlet	scurry	scar	scan	scone	
scarce	scald	scold	scorch	school	scheme	schooner
split	splinter	splendid				
squad	squat	squid	squash			

1 Which **list** word?
I am a sailing ship with two or more masts. ______________
I am a place in which education takes place. ______________
I am a sea creature with a soft body and tentacles. ______________
I am a crouching position. ______________
I am a plan. ______________
I am the result of damaged skin tissue. ______________

2 Write the **list** words, beginning with ***squ***, in alphabetical order.
____

3 Use a dictionary to help you find and write the difference in meaning of scold and scald.
scold ______________________ scald ______________________

4 Replace the underlined words in these sentences with **list** or **challenge** words.
The small group (______________) of scouts attended their first jamboree.
Greedy Michael stole the last light plain cake (______________) from the pantry.
It only took a few seconds for Mum to remove the small sliver of wood (____________) from Melanie's finger.
'It is unfortunate that hairy-nosed wombats are becoming rare (______________),' stated Professor Petersen.
We were fearful that the water in the pot would burn with hot liquid (______________) poor little Jenny.

Strategy

Make word sums.
For example:
squ + ash
splen + did
splin + ter
splint + er
spl + in + ter.

Word Building

Add ***er*** and ***ing*** to the following words and then write a sentence containing any two of your new words. (Remember that these words need to have the last **consonant** doubled before ***er*** or ***ing*** is added.)

split ______________ ______________ squat ______________ ______________
scan ______________ ______________

____
____
____

Challenge

scuba	scorpion
squalid	scholar
splendour	squirrel

Home Study Unit 20

An ape's an ape, a varlet's a varlet though they be clad in silk or scarlet.

(Proverb)

1 Draw a picture of a school of squid *or* a squad of scurrying scorpions.

2 Use the ***sc*** (but not ***sch***) words, from the **list**, to complete this Wordsearch.

S	S	C	A	R	C	E	S
C	S	S	S	S	E	S	C
A	C	C	C	C	P	C	O
H	A	A	U	A	C	E	N
C	T	V	S	R	R	T	E
R	T	E	C	H	R	S	D
O	E	L	S	N	A	Y	D
C	R	S	A	C	S	C	L
S	S	C	O	L	D	R	A
C	S	R	S	C	A	P	C
S	C	A	R	L	E	T	S

WORD history

Scuba is actually an **acronym** (a word made from the first letters of other words).

It stands for Self Contained Underwater Breathing Apparatus.

3 Which **list** or **challenge** words? ______________ ______________

Word Knowledge

1 Which of the following animals' movements might be described as a scurry?

elephant crab ant tortoise whale beetle rabbit ______________________________

2 Match these **challenge** words with definitions.

one who studies ______________ self-contained underwater breathing apparatus ______________

dirty and mean ______________ a lobster-like arachnid ______________

wonder ______________ small bush-tailed animal ______________

General Knowledge

1 According to legend, to which band of outlaws did Will Scarlet belong? ______________

2 In the poem 'Waltzing Matilda' by Banjo Paterson, how many squatters attempted to capture the jolly swagman? ______________

3 What is the geographical area consisting of Norway, Sweden, Denmark (and sometimes Finland and Iceland)? ______________

th tw dw wh as in thaw twine dwell whim

Your List

thaw	Thursday	thirsty	thought	thorough	theory	twist	twelfth
twine	twirl	twelve	twilight	twitch	twinge	twenty	whenever
dwarf	dwell	dwindle	whisper	whirl	whim	whisk	whisker

1 Which **list** words rhyme? ______________ ______________

2 Which **list** word(s)…?

relate to numbers ______________ ______________ ______________

is a day of the week ______________ involves a body movement ______________

grows on a cat ______________ might you find in a fairytale ______________

3 Which **list** words are disguised in these **acrostics**?

The walrus is swimming tenaciously. ______________

Do wizards enchant little lizards? ______________

Ten walkers entered new territory yesterday. ______________

The happy alligator won. ______________

Strategy

Look for smaller words.
For example:
thorough = rough
dwindle = in win wind
twinge = in win wing.

4 Write your own **acrostics**, using these **list** words.

dwarf d ______________ w ______________ a ______________ r ______________ f ______________

twine t ______________ w ______________ i ______________ n ______________ e ______________

5 Write Yes or No.

Does a thermometer have a whisker? ______________

Does an ice cube dwindle as it thaws? ______________

Is it thoroughly dark at twilight time? ______________

6 Write one sentence containing three of the *wh* words.

____

____

Word Building

1 Add the **suffix** or **prefix** shown to make new words.

thought + (ful) ______________ thorough + (fare) ______________

(blood) + thirsty ______________ thought + (less) ______________

when + (ever) ______________

Challenge

thorax
thermometer
whimsical

2 Add *ing* to the following **list** words.

twinge ______________ dwindle ______________ twitch ______________

thaw ______________ twirl ______________

twist ______________ whirl ______________

Home Study Unit 21

Little boy kneels at the foot of his bed,
Droops on little hands, little gold head;
Hush! Hush! whisper who dares!
Christopher Robin is saying his prayers.
(A. A. Milne)

1 Use the clues to complete this Crossword with **list** words.

Across	**Down**
1 idea	1 melt
5 talk quietly	2 week day
6 live	3 bristle
8 a number	4 spin rapidly
9 thin string	7 wind together

2 Which **list** words...?

contain double **consonants** ____________

begin with a capital letter ____________

end with *e* ____________ ____________ ____________ ____________

end with the same letter they begin with ____________ ____________ ____________

3 Which **list** words mean...?

momentary pain ____________ time between afternoon and dark ____________

gradually get smaller ____________ fancy ____________

Word Knowledge

Group the following words according to sound and movement.

twitter tweet twiddle twirl twitch twist twinge whirl whisk whisper

Sound	**Movement**		
____________	____________	____________	____________
____________	____________	____________	
____________	____________	____________	

WORD history

Thor was the Viking god of thunder.

Which day do you think might have been Thor's day?

General Knowledge

1 Who are we? We are two characters whose only difference is our names. We featured in one of Lewis Carroll's most famous books. ____________

2 How many different animals make up the Chinese horoscope? ____________

3 Which **challenge** word has been formed from the Greek word *thermos* (hot) and *metron* (measure)? ____________

Classroom Unit 22 ct ft pt as in fact soft erupt

Your List

fact	pact	exact	erect	reject	collect	affect	object	reflect
perfect	respect	select	correct	eject	attract	aircraft	neglect	receipt
loft	lift	raft	soft	craft	drift	swift	compact	extract
erupt	script	tempt	attempt	accept	abrupt	prompt	except	extinct

1 Join the beginnings and endings shown to form nine **list** words.

tem	li	prom	ft
fa	swi	respe	pt
perfe	exa	scri	ct

______________ ______________ ______________
______________ ______________ ______________
______________ ______________ ______________

2 Match these meanings with **list** words.

an agreement ______________ gather together ______________ try ______________
sudden ______________ look up to ______________ upper room ______________

3 Write one interesting sentence containing: receipt, exact and neglect.

____

4 Use **list** words to fill in the gaps in these sentences.

The mountaineers decided to make one final ______________ at climbing to the summit before dark.

The company requested ______________ payments from its customers.

After reading the ______________ the famous actor decided she could not do justice to the role.

The history professor reeled off one ______________ after another to his students.

Look
Say
Cover
Write
Check

Word Building

1 Add the **suffix *ion*** to the following words.

except ______________ eject ______________ correct ______________ collect ______________
reflect ______________ object ______________ perfect ______________ extinct ______________

Use appropriate words from above in these sentences.

The residents had a strong ______________ to the ______________ of their garbage on Sundays.

The brilliant ______________ of the exploding bomb's light, caused the earlier ______________ of the pilot from his jet plane.

The politician quickly made a ______________ to his speech after the new unemployment figures were shown.

Challenge

disrupt deflect
verdict manuscript

Home Study Unit 22

> The race is not to the swift,
> nor the battle to the strong.
> (Ecclesiastes 9:11)

1 Write the six **list** words that can be formed from the name Cape Firstly. (Letters cannot be used twice in one word.)

______________ ______________ ______________

______________ ______________ ______________

2 Which **list** words are **antonyms** (opposites) for…?

hard ______________ slow ______________ incorrect ______________

accept ______________ discourage ______________

3 Which **list** words?

stamps, coins, aluminium cans, footy cards ______________

mirror, water, the moon, glass ______________

Mt St Helens, Mt Vesuvius, Krakatau (Krakatoa), molten lava ______________

macramé, origami, papier-maché, embroidery ______________

4 Write **list** or **challenge** words in these Wordframes.

Word Knowledge

Match the words on the left with a suitable definition.

affection	pay no attention to
extinction	closely packed together
deflection	something that throws things out of order
extraction	warm feelings of love
neglect	a decision or judgement
verdict	being wiped out; ceasing to exist
disruption	taking out
compact	movement away from something

General Knowledge

1 What do the dodo, thylacine, moa and stegosaurus have in common?

____

2 The modern explorer Thor Heyerdahl drifted across the Pacific Ocean on his raft *Kon Tiki*. What material was the raft made from? ______________

3 Which fictional detective lived at 221B Baker Street, London? ______________

Consonant blends

Your List

tact	direct	restrict	shaft	apt	shift	dwell	whiff
twinkle	tweezers	tweed	scalp	squatter	splash	splutter	squadron

1 Select three of the **list** words to write in one interesting sentence.

____

2 Write in alphabetical order: twinkle, tact, tweed, tweezers.

____

3 Match these definitions with **list** words.

a rough woollen cloth ______________

skin of the head where hair grows ______________

suitable or appropriate ______________

someone who lives somewhere without permission ______________

a wisp or slight puff ______________

a sense of the correct time to do or say something ______________

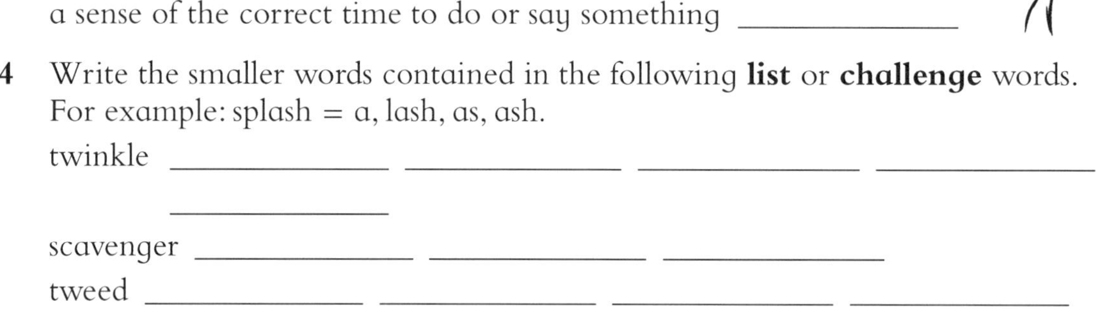

4 Write the smaller words contained in the following **list** or **challenge** words.
For example: splash = a, lash, as, ash.

twinkle ______________ ______________ ______________ ______________ ______________

scavenger ______________ ______________ ______________

tweed ______________ ______________ ______________ ______________

Word Building

Add the **suffix** ***ion*** to the following and then write each in a sentence.

direct ______________________________________

____

restrict ______________________________________

____

intercept ______________________________________

____

Challenge

conscript	intercept	deft
scavenger	schedule	scholarship

Look for smaller words.
For example:
dwells = ell, we, well.

Home Study Review

1 Draw a spluttering squatter *or* a squadron of tweezers.

Twinkle, Twinkle little bat!
How I wonder what you're at!
Up above the world you fly!
Like a teatray in the sky!
(Lewis Carroll)

WORD history

A scholarship is a sum of money won by a student to help pay for school or university fees.
The word 'scholar' comes from the Latin word *schola*, which means school.

Classroom Review 2

2 Which **list** words?

__ h a __ __ __ w __ __ __ l __ __ e __ t __ __ c t __ __ __ __ t t __ __

3 Use a **list** word in each of the following sentences.

The miner followed the vertical ______________ one kilometre underground.

The gatekeeper's job was to ______________ the spectators to the correct entrance.

As we approached the hut a ______________ of smoke rose gently from the chimney.

Mr Beggs used great ______________ in handling the tricky situation.

Word Knowledge

Use a dictionary to help you write the definitions of these **challenge** words.

scavenger ______________________________

conscript ______________________________

intercept ______________________________

deft ______________________________

schedule ______________________________

General Knowledge

1 Were young men conscripted into the Australian army during the Vietnam War? ______________

2 What sort of person dwells in or would have dwelt in:

a wigwam or tepee? ______________ a kraal? ______________ an igloo? ______________

3 Which **list** word describes what the following creatures have in common: crows, hyenas, buzzards? ______________________

Classroom Unit 23

Plurals: s sh ch x z as in chorus thrush patch hoax buzz

Your List

chorus	switch	launch	success	hoax
bonus	patch	hunch	witness	index
thrush	stitch	speech	fortress	buzz
leash	stretch	screech	harness	
	sketch	sandwich		

RULE: When **nouns** end with *s*, *ss*, *sh*, *ch*, *x* or *z*, the **plural** is formed by adding *es*.

1 Re-write the words in the **list** box, making all of them **plurals**.

2 Which **list plurals**?

guesses ________________ open motor boats ________________

high piercing sounds ________________ leather fittings for horses ________________

parts of songs that are repeated after the verses ________________

lists of subjects and names to be found in books ________________

3 Which **list plurals** best fit into the gaps in these sentences?

Before beginning vigorous exercise, athletes usually warm up their muscles with a series of ______________.

We were woken by the early morning song of a family of ____________ on the lawn.

The tricksters had succeeded in carrying out many ____________ before being found out by the police.

Word Building

Complete the following table.

	Add *ed*	**Add *ing***	**Plural**
buzz	buzzed	buzzing	buzzes
harness	__________	__________	__________
screech	__________	__________	__________
stitch	__________	__________	__________
witness	__________	__________	__________
switch	__________	__________	__________

Challenge

minuses processes wirelesses recesses excesses

Home Study Unit 23

A wandering minstrel I—
A thing of shreds and patches,
of ballads, songs and snatches,
A dreaming lullaby!
(W. S. Gilbert)

1 Find the list **plurals** shown in this Wordsearch.

bonuses
choruses
fortresses
hoaxes
hunches
launches
screeches
sketches
stitches
switches

S	T	I	T	C	H	S	E	S	N	C
E	H	H	O	A	X	E	S	H	U	H
H	B	F	S	E	E	C	H	S	H	E
C	O	O	C	R	T	H	E	K	U	S
T	A	R	N	I	C	H	C	E	N	E
I	X	T	W	U	C	S	W	T	C	H
W	E	R	S	E	S	S	A	C	H	C
S	S	E	E	H	E	E	T	H	E	T
F	O	R	T	R	E	S	S	E	S	I
S	C	S	T	R	E	T	E	S	H	T
S	C	H	O	R	U	S	E	S	E	S
S	W	L	A	U	N	C	H	E	S	E

2 Which **list plurals**?

______________ ______________ ______________

WORD history

The first sandwiches were eaten by the fourth Earl of Sandwich. The Earl refused to leave the gambling table to eat lunch. His cook decided to prepare something the Earl could eat while gambling, and so placed the slice of meat between two pieces of bread.

Word Knowledge

Which **challenge** words?

radios ______________ subtractions ______________ hollows ______________

extreme amounts ______________ series of actions taken ______________

Select a **challenge** word and write it in a sentence.

____

____

General Knowledge

1 What are we? We are monotremes (egg-laying mammals). We live in rivers and billabongs. We are noted for our strange appearance. Early white settlers thought we were a practical joke.

____

2 What are we? We are large sea mammals. We have tusks when we are full grown and we live in Arctic regions. ______________________

Classroom Unit 24 Plurals: y as in melody

Your List

ability	charity	mystery	library	melody
cavity	misery	quarry	nursery	laundry
lottery	penalty	luxury	tragedy	quantity

RULE: When **nouns** end in a **consonant** and ***y***, the plural is formed by dropping the ***y*** and adding ***ies***. Example: cherry—cherries.

1 Re-write the words in the **list** box, making them all **plural**.

2 Use a dictionary to help you define the following. (Hint: You may need to change the words back to singular first.)

tragedies ______

quarries ______

cavities ______

3 Which **list plurals** best fit in these word groups?

Loch Ness, Bermuda Triangle, UFOs ______

Tattslotto, Tattersalls, Pools ______

Red Cross, Red Shield, St Vincent de Paul, Smith Family ______

4 Write a suitable **list plural** in the gaps in these sentences.

We tried many ______ but still could not find the books we needed.

During the game the Socceroos received ten ______ from the referee.

After visiting several ______ we found the plant that we wanted.

The ocean cruise ship contained all of the ______ that the passengers could ask for.

Word Building

Complete:

an ability, many ______

one melody, a chorus of ______

one laundry, a row of ______

one cavity, many ______

a quarry, two ______

one quantity, several ______

Challenge

casualties embassies harmonies universities

> The sweetest melodies
> Are those that are by distance made more sweet.
> (William Wordsworth)

1 Complete these **list plurals**.

__ b __ __ __ __ __ __ __ __   __ r __ g __ __ __ __ __ __

__ __ x __ __ __ __ __ __   __ av __ __ __ __ __ __

2 Write these **list plurals** in alphabetical order:
mysteries, melodies, laundries, lotteries and libraries.

____

3 Which **list plurals**?

skills ________________ raffles for money ________________

large open stone pits ________________ rooms for washing clothes ________________

places where books are stored and borrowed ________________

places where plants are sold or babies are cared for ________________

4 Write one interesting sentence containing: mysteries and libraries.

____

____

WORD history

In Latin *libraria* is the word for a bookseller's shop.
In Latin *nutrire* is the word for a place to nourish children.
In Greek *melos* is the word for a song or rhythmical chant.
In Greek *tragoidia* is the word for a goat's song.
In Latin *poena* is the word for punishment.
In French/Latin *cavitas* is the word for hollow.
In Latin *universitas* is the word for a group of teachers and students.
Can you see which **list** words these may be related to?

Word Knowledge

1 Make a list of any special abilities you may have.
For example: drawing, sport.

____

____

2 Which **challenge** words?

places of higher education ________________

those injured or killed ________________

pleasing combinations of musical notes ________________

offices and houses of ambassadors ________________

General Knowledge

1 What do the following have in common?
Oxford, Melbourne, Monash, Macquarie, Cambridge, Yale, Harvard ________________

2 Who is the most likely person to deal with oral cavities? ________________

3 Who wrote the following tragedies? *King Lear, Julius Caesar, Hamlet, Othello, Macbeth, Romeo and Juliet* ________________

Classroom Unit 25 Plurals: y after a vowel

Your List

chimney	storey	subway
volley	pulley	journey
decoy	buoy	highway
valley	trolley	

RULE: When **nouns** end in a **vowel** and *y*, the **plural** is formed by adding *s*.

1 Re-write the words in the **list** box, making them all **plurals**.

2 Which **list plurals?**

3 Write one interesting sentence containing any two **list** words.

4 Which **list plurals**?

You might use us in a game of tennis. ________

A hunter may use us. ________

Customers would use us at a supermarket. ________

Rivers might be found winding through us. ________

We could be found in a busy bay or harbour. ________

Word Building

Make compound plurals by adding the beginnings in Group A to the word *ways*.

Group A

free
sub
high + ways
cause
by
passage

Challenge

attorneys quays ploys

Home Study Unit 25

> The moon has a face like the clock in the hall;
> She shines on thieves on the garden wall,
> On streets and fields and harbour quays,
> And birdies asleep in the forks of the trees.
> (R. L. Stevenson)

1 Complete this Wordcross using **list plurals**.

Down
smoke flues

Across
1 lures
2 major roads
3 hand-drawn trucks
4 floating markers

WORD history
Subway comes from the words 'sub' (meaning under) and 'way' (meaning road or path). Can you think of more words that begin with 'sub'?
Can you think of more words ending with 'way'?

2 Which **list** or **challenge** words match these **homonyms**?
boys ______________ keys ______________
stories ______________

3 Draw trolleys full of buoys *or* decoys on chimneys.

4 Write True or False for these sentences.
Can you take long journeys through subways? ______________
Are decoys used to clean chimneys? ______________
Do tennis players have long volleys? ______________

Word Knowledge

Use a dictionary to find the meanings of the three **challenge** words and then write one sentence using any two of the words to show their meanings.

____

____

____

General Knowledge

1 How many journeys did Captain Cook make to the South Seas before being killed in Hawaii (Sandwich Islands)? ______________

2 Which Australian highways are numbered 1 and 31? ______________

3 Which **list plural** would best match…?
Yarra, Mitta, Barossa, Hunter, Ovens ______________

Plurals: f fe as in leaf wife

Your List

leaf	loaf	thief	half	self	calf
shelf	wolf		life	wife	knife

RULE: For some **nouns** which end with *f* or *fe*, the **plural** is formed by changing the *f* or *fe* to *v* and then adding *es*.

1 Re-write the words in the **list** box as **plurals**.

2 Select a suitable **list plural** to write in each of the following sentences.
The police arrested the ______________ at the scene of the crime.
During the night we could hear the howling of ______________ in the distance.
The players and their husbands and ______________ were invited to the after-match dinner.
It is said that cats have nine ______________.
Two ______________ make one whole.

3 Write in alphabetical order the **plurals** of: life, leaf, loaf, wolf and wife.
____

4 Which **list plurals** are these?
k n _ _ _ _   s h _ _ _ _ _   t h _ _ _ _ _

Word Building

The following words, when changed to **plurals**, can be written with either *ves* or *s*.

Hoof = hoofs or hooves; scarf = scarfs or scarves; wharf = wharfs or wharves.

Write the **plural** (either form) of each of these three words in sentences.

____
____
____
____
____
____
____
____
____

Challenge

sheaves

Home Study Unit 26

> Lives of great men remind us
> We can make our lives sublime
> And, departing, leave behind us
> Footprints on the sands of time.
> (Henry Wadsworth Longfellow)

1 Which **list** words?

_______________ _______________ _______________ _______________

2 Which **list plurals** are best associated with the following?

quarters, eighths, thirds _______________ lambs, piglets, foals _______________

burglars, robbers, pirates _______________ trees, branches, roots _______________

books, ornaments, DVDs _______________ spoons, forks, teaspoons _______________

3 Write one interesting sentence containing: leaves and wolves.

____

____

4 Which **list plurals** fit into these Wordframes?

Word Knowledge

Find the meaning of the **challenge** word and then write it in an interesting sentence.

____

____

General Knowledge

1 What do the following have in common?
switchblade, dagger, hunting, carving, butter, pen, Stanley _______________

2 What do the following people have in common?
Robin Hood, Captain Moonlight, Ned Kelly, The Great Train Robber

____

3 True or False? Wolves are wild dogs found in outback Australia. _______________

Plurals: no change

Your List

sheep	deer	fish	moose	trout	athletics
squid	salmon	corps	craft	aircraft	reindeer

RULE: Some **nouns** have the same spelling whether they are singular or **plural**. These are your **list** and **challenge** words for this unit.

1 Complete the following sentences.

The shearer had already shorn one hundred ____________ by the time we arrived at the shed.

Many ____________ can be caught in the mountain stream including ____________ and ____________.

The ____________ stretched out their tentacles towards the unsuspecting ____________.

At the beginning of the yacht race many spectator ____________ could be seen on the water.

Army ____________ from six different nations took part in the exercise.

The ____________ had been bred at the farm so that their antlers could be used.

During our camping trip in Canada we saw many large ____________ wandering the mountains.

2 Which **list plurals** rhyme with…?

poor ____________ famine ____________

3 Which **list** words contain smaller words which mean…?

not in ____________ floating platform ____________

not out ____________ exists ____________

4 Write one interesting sentence containing: fish and craft.

____

____

5 Write a sentence in which the word *fish* is used in its **plural** form.

Note: the **plural** of fish can be fish or fishes, although fish is more commonly used.

____

Word Building

What am I? A shepherd might look after us. ____________

What are we? We tow a sleigh. ____________

What does ANZAC stand for?

A ____________ N ____________ Z ____________ A ____________ C ____________

Challenge

stationery

Home Study Unit 27

> The tiny fish enjoy themselves in the sea
> Quick little splinters of life,
> their little lives are fun for them in the sea.
> (D. H. Lawrence)

1 Which **list** words mean…?
large North American deer ______________
large pink-fleshed fish ______________
units of soldiers ______________
freshwater fish (brown or rainbow) ______________
soft-bodied sea animals with ten tentacles ______________

2 Which **list** words?

______________ ______________ ______________

3 Which **list** words fit into these Wordframes?

4 Use a dictionary to help you write the definition of the **challenge** word.

____

Which word is a **homonym** of the **challenge** word? ______________
Write the word's definition here. ______________________________

Word Knowledge

Write as many athletics events as you can think of.

____
____
____
____

WORD history

'Corps' comes from the French phrase *corps d'armee*, which means army unit. The word is also used to describe other types of units such as press corps, medical corps and diplomatic corps.

General Knowledge

1 How many tentacles do ten squid have? ______________

2 What do the following have in common: Cessna, F18, Learjet, Boeing 747, Zero, Stealth Bomber? ______________________________

3 How many different kinds of fish can you list ? ______________________________
____

Classroom Unit 28

Plurals: words that are always plural

Your List

clothes	police	pants	trousers	stairs	pyjamas
scissors	scales	shears	cattle	glasses	binoculars

Ask: does the word look right?

RULE: These words are always written and spoken in **plural** form.

1 Write the **list** words in alphabetical order.

____

____

2 Which **list** plurals contain smaller words that mean…?

listening organs ___________ a feline ___________ Scottish girls ___________

3 Which **list** words can be used as **synonyms** for these…?

trousers ___________ steps ___________ spectacles ___________

clippers ___________ balances ___________

4 Which **list** words?

___________ ___________ ___________ ___________

5 Write one interesting sentence containing any three **list** words.

____

____

Word Building

Match the words in the two groups to form new **compound words**. (Words may be used twice.)

Group A

sun clothes police

up down nail

\+

Group B

stairs line scissors

officer glasses

____

____

Challenge

pliers spectacles breeches

> Out on the board the old shearer stands
> Grasping his shears in his long bony hands.
> (Anon.)

1 Which **list** words?

We are used to clip wool from sheep and goats. ______________

We are two-legged outer garments covering from the waist to the ankles. ______________

We are employed by the government to uphold the law. ______________

We are a set of steps leading to an upper or lower floor. ______________

We are simple balances. ______________

We are lenses in a frame used to improve eyesight. ______________

2 Which **list** words?

__ l __ t h __ __   __ __ __ __ __ __ l a r s   p __ __ __ m __ s   s __ __ s s __ __ s

3 Draw police wearing blue trousers *or* cattle walking upstairs.

Word Knowledge

Which **list** or **challenge** words?

night clothes ______________   field glasses ______________   knee length trousers ______________

Write each **challenge** word in a sentence.

____

____

____

General Knowledge

1 What is the name given to the piece of equipment with a name coming from the Latin words *bini* (meaning two together) and *oculus* (meaning eye)? ______________

2 With which cultural group would you associate the following clothes?

yashmak ______________   sarong ______________

sari ______________   kimono ______________   burka ______________

WORD history

Which **list** or **challenge** word comes from the Latin word *speculan* meaning to spy out or watch?

Classroom Unit 29

Plurals: o after a consonant

Your List

tomato	motto	potato	hero	echo	cargo	dingo
mosquito	torpedo	tornado	buffalo	volcano	mango	flamingo

____
____
____

RULE: When **nouns** end in a **consonant** and then ***o***, the **plural** is formed by adding ***es***.

Strategy

Add *es*.

1 Re-write the words in the **list** box as **plurals**.

2 Which **list** words mean…?

kind of wild oxen ______________
blood-sucking insects ______________
phrases of good advice ______________
Australian wild dogs ______________
long-legged birds ______________
brave people ______________
repeated sounds ______________
underwater explosives ______________
goods carried on ships ______________
juicy fruits ______________

3 Which **list plurals** contain smaller words that mean…?

small carpet ______________ pan ______________ ripped ______________

4 Write a suitable **list plural** in each of the gaps in these sentences.

Grandad grows ______________ and ______________ in his vegetable garden.
Mt Vesuvius and Mt Etna are two ______________ that have erupted.
During the war many ships lost their ______________ after being hit by ______________ from submarines.
The buzz of ______________, ______________ around the room each night.

5 Use **list plurals** to complete these groups.

flies, bees, butterflies ______________
mountains, hills, craters ______________
cattle, oxen, bullocks ______________
beans, tomatoes, cabbages ______________
numbats, kangaroos, koalas ______________
storks, cranes, brolgas ______________

Challenge

vetoes avocadoes

> Blow, bugle, blow,
> set the wild echoes flying,
> Blow, bugle, blow;
> answer, echoes dying, dying, dying.
> (Alfred Lord Tennyson)

1 Find the words on the left in the following Wordsearch.

cargoes
dingoes
echoes
heroes
mosquitoes
mottoes
potatoes
tomatoes
volcanoes
buffaloes

V	P	O	C	L	C	O	E	S	D	M	D	I	N	G	O	S
T	O	M	A	T	O	E	S	P	I	N	O	E	S	E	H	N
T	T	O	R	N	T	E	C	H	N	T	O	T	E	S	C	M
O	A	P	G	M	O	T	T	O	G	S	E	O	T	T	O	E
M	T	O	O	R	R	P	O	V	O	L	C	A	N	O	E	S
A	O	T	E	T	P	T	A	E	E	C	H	O	E	S	E	S
T	E	H	S	V	A	S	M	O	S	Q	U	I	T	O	E	S
S	S	B	U	F	F	A	L	O	E	S	H	E	R	S	O	E

2 Write in alphabetical order: torpedoes, tornadoes, buffaloes, cargoes and tomatoes.

____

3 Use a dictionary to help you define the following **list** or **challenge plurals**.

vetoes ______________________________

mottoes ______________________________

Word Knowledge

Match the list of **adjectives** (describing words) below with these **list plurals**.

echoes ______________________________

volcanoes ______________________________

heroes ______________________________

violent	ringing	courageous	furious	fiery
resonant	gallant	hollow	valiant	reverberating
intrepid	explosive			

WORD history

volcanoes from Latin *vulcanus*—Roman god of fire
tornadoes from Spanish *tronada*—thunderstorm
mosquitoes (a Spanish word) from Latin *musca*—a fly
potatoes from Spanish *patata* —white potato
tomatoes from Spanish *tomate* from West Indian *tomatl*—'love apple'

General Knowledge

1 What name is given to underwater missiles fired from a submarine? ________________

2 What do the following have in common?
Mt Etna, Mt Vesuvius, Mauna Kea, Mt St Helens, Mauna Loa ________________

3 What do mangoes and avocadoes have in common? ________________

Classroom Unit 30

Plurals: o after a vowel

Your List

ratio	trio	folio	studio
dynamo	kimono	photo	auto
banjo	patio	tempo	soprano
kilo	rodeo	radio	piano
video	cuckoo	cockatoo	kangaroo

RULE: Usually if **nouns** end with a **vowel** and then *o*, the **plural** is formed by adding *s*. For example: trios. The same rule applies where the word that ends with *o* is of foreign origin (for example: kimonos), a musical term (for example: arpeggios) or an abbreviated word (for example: pianos).

1 Re-write the words in the **list** box as **plurals**.

2 Which **list plurals** mean…?

Japanese gowns ____________ short for photographs ____________
workrooms ____________ outdoor living areas ____________
groups of three ____________ short for kilograms ____________

3 Write a **list plural** in each of the Wordframes.

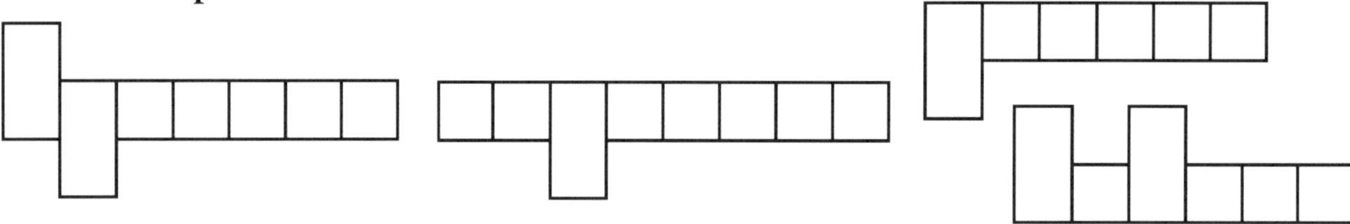

4 Write the **list plurals** that are living creatures.

____

5 Which **list plurals** best fit the following?

visual tapes ____________ shows for cowboys' skills ____________
communications instruments ____________ instruments for strumming ____________
speeds of music ____________ relationships between two amounts ____________
electricity producing machines ____________ highest singing voices ____________

Word Building

The following words have been abbreviated.

Write them in full.

photos ____________
autos ____________
kilos ____________

Just add *s*.

Challenge
fiascos

Home Study Unit 30

The strongest creature for its size
  But least equipped for combat
That dwells beneath Australian skies
  Is Weary Will the Wombat.
He digs his homestead underground,
  He's neither shrewd nor clever;
For kangaroos can leap and bound
  But wombats dig forever.
(A. B. 'Banjo' Paterson)

1 Use the **list plurals** to fill the gaps in these sentences.
During the opera the voices of the __________ stood out above all others.
The stockrider now made a living competing in __________ around country NSW.
Electric lights at the campsite were powered by huge __________.

2 Write in alphabetical order: folios, photos, autos, trios and videos.

____

3 Which **list** or **challenge plurals** contain smaller words that could also be names of people?

____

4 Write any three **list plurals** in one interesting sentence.

____

____

Word Knowledge

Use a dictionary to help you write a definition for *fiascos*.

____

____

General Knowledge

1 What are we?
We are worn in Japan. We are long, loose robes with wide sleeves and a sash. __________

2 What is the name given for the text of operas? Is it sopranos, concertos, librettos, tempos or rondos? __________

3 Which of the following are not marsupials? cuckoos, cockatoos, kangaroos, wallabies, koalas, taipans __________

WORD history

kimonos—Japanese robes
autos—short for automobiles (*auto*—self, *mobile*—propelling)
pianos—short for *pianoforte* from Italian (soft and loud)
radios—short for radio telegraphy—from Latin (*radius*—ray, *tele*—far off, *graphos*—writing)
videos—from Latin (*video* meaning I see)

Plurals

Classroom Review 3

Your List

circus	victory	hutch	prefix	princess
kidney	squid	latch	survey	search
suffix	success	shelf	scissors	clash
injury	ranch	memory	wife	sheep
tornado	radio			

1 Re-write the words in the **list** box as **plurals** under the rules to which they belong. These new words are your **list** words for this unit.

When **nouns** end with ***s***, ***ss***, ***sh***, ***ch***, ***x*** or ***z***, add ***es*** to form **plurals**.

For **nouns** that end with ***y*** following a **consonant**, form the **plural** by dropping the ***y*** and adding ***ies***.

For **nouns** ending with ***y*** following a **vowel**, form the **plural** by adding ***s***.

For some words ending with ***f*** or ***fe***, form the **plural** by changing the ***f*** or ***fe*** to ***v*** and add ***es***.

Some **nouns** have the same spelling whether singular or **plural**.

Some words are nearly always used in **plural** form.

For **nouns** ending with ***o*** following a **consonant**, form the **plural** by adding ***es***.

Usually **nouns** ending with ***o*** following a **vowel** become **plural** by adding ***s***.

Word Building

Add the **prefixes** or **suffixes** shown to form new words.

Group A			Group B	
sub	anti		operate	star
super	re		head	clockwise
co	trans	+	marine	veil
fore	un		wind	port
ous	able		comfort	motor
ist	ful		courage	success

Challenge

equinoxes sphinxes ratios concertos

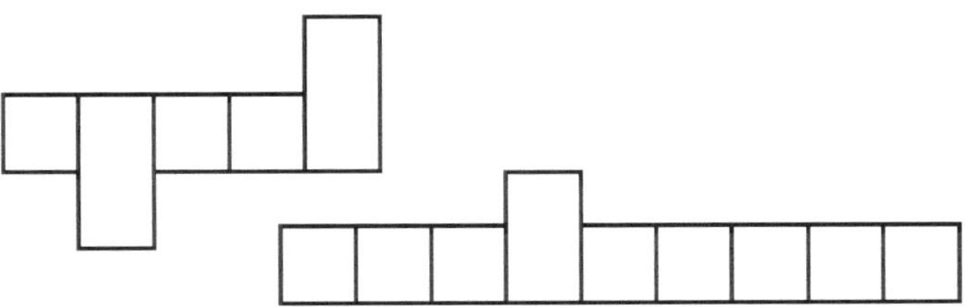

Home Study Review

He was drifting down in the
Eighty drought
with a mob that could scarcely
creep.
(When the kangaroos by the
thousand starve,
it is tough on the travelling
sheep.)

(A. B. 'Banjo' Paterson)

Classroom Review 3

1 Which **list plurals** fit into these Wordframes?

2 Write the list **plurals** that:
contain double **vowels** ______________
contain double **consonants** ______________ ______________ ______________ ______________
contain more than three **vowels** ______________ ______________ ______________ ______________
contain less than three **vowels** ______________ ______________ ______________ ______________ ______________ ______________ ______________ ______________ ______________ ______________ ______________

3 Draw the result of clashes of squid.

4 Which list **plurals**?
We are organs. ______________
We can be homes for animals. ______________
We are word endings. ______________

Word Knowledge

Match the following **prefixes** and **suffixes** with their meanings.

Prefixes	Meanings	Suffixes	Meanings
circum	across	ful	office or rank
pre	around	hood	state of being
milli	self	ist	full of
sub	under	ship	a person who performs
trans	thousand		
auto	before		

General Knowledge

1 Which bean-shaped organs filter waste from the human body? ______________

2 What are all the following?
Flying Fruit Flies, Oz, Ashton's, Cirque du Soleil ______________

3 How many equinoxes are there in one year? ______________

Homonyms—Homophones

Your List

bough	bow		mourning	morning	thrown	throne	
dew	due		veil	vale	presence	presents	
scene	seen		weather	whether	aloud	allowed	
their	there	they're	principle	principal	to	too	two

1 Circle the correct word in these sentences.

The family waited patiently for the (presence/presents) of the prince before they began unwrapping their (presence/presents).

The heavy (due/dew) on the grass was (due/dew) to the drop in the temperature overnight.

During the performance the children were not (allowed/aloud) to talk (allowed/aloud).

A (veil/vale) of mist descended upon the tiny village at the northern end of the (veil/vale).

The tourists gasped at the wonderful (scene/seen), a view many had never (scene/seen) before.

'(They're/their/there) over (they're/their/there) preparing for (they're/their/there) next game,' reported the assistant coach.

2 Which **list** words mean…?

feeling or showing sorrow ______________ a tree limb ______________

a royal person's seat ______________ the time before noon ______________

the front part of a ship or to bend body forwards ______________ tossed ______________

3 Write one interesting sentence containing: to, too and two.

____

____

Remember: to = in the direction of/as far as too = also/as well as two = the number

Word Building

1 From which **list** or **challenge** words do the following come?

scenery ______________ twice ______________

principality ______________ allowable ______________

2 Add ***ed*** to the following words and then write each new word in a sentence.

weather ____

bow ____

veil ____

Make up memory triggers. For example: Have you seen the scene? The king has thrown his throne. You are not allowed to talk aloud.

Challenge

suite sweet

Home Study Unit 31

> There was a Door to which I found no key;
> There was a Veil past which I could not see.
> (Edward Fitzgerald)

1 Complete the following Wordcross. (The clues are **homophones** of the answers.)

Down
principle

Across
1 presents
2 whether
3 scene
4 vale
5 aloud

2 Write the following words in sentences.
their ____________________
they're ____________________
there ____________________

3 Which **list** words?
_ h _ _ w _   _ _ r _ n _   _ _ w   _ o _ g _

Word Knowledge

1 Find the definitions of each of the **challenge** words in a dictionary and then write each in a sentence.

____
____
____
____

WORD history
The Latin word *princeps* means first, most important or chief. Which **list** words have come from this Latin word?

2 Match **list** words with these groups of **synonyms**.

branch, limb ____________________
gifts, donations ____________________
tossed, hurled, cast ____________________
valley, dale, dell, gully ____________________
view, landscape, vista ____________________
owing, outstanding, unpaid ____________________

General Knowledge

1 Who is the principal of your school? ____________________

2 What do sailors call the following parts of a ship?
the front ____________________ the back ____________________
the left side ____________________ the right side ____________________

3 Who is next in line to the throne of England? ____________________

Classroom Unit **32**

Homonyms—Homographs

Your List

fast	novel	palm	foil	scale	stable
stalk	steer	toll	count	grate	hatch

1 Match the **list** words with the following definitions.

to ring slowly ______________

to add up ______________

inside of the hand ______________

to guide ______________

a long imaginative story ______________

tall tree ______________

able to move quickly ______________

metal grid ______________

break out of an egg ______________

time without food ______________

stem of a plant ______________

climb ______________

stop from being successful ______________

size, compared to something else ______________

new or different ______________

thin metal sheets ______________

a deck, floor or ceiling opening ______________

a horse's home ______________

a noble person ______________

rub together making a rough sound ______________

a fee paid to use a road or bridge ______________

to follow quietly ______________

male cow ______________

firm and steady ______________

light thin sword ______________

thin plate on fish ______________

2 Write suitable **list** words in the gaps in these sentences.

The main characters in the famous ______________ were the prince and a poor little boy.

Children were asked to wipe their muddy feet on the metal ______________ before entering the building.

The scientists waited impatiently to see what sort of creature would ______________ from the strange egg.

Word Building

1 Add the word part shown to form new words.

fast + (en) ________________

(dis) + count ________________

(bean) + stalk ________________

novel + (ty) ________________

(full) + scale ________________

(break) + fast ________________

2 Write one of your new words in an interesting sentence.

____

____

____

Challenge

poker poach

Home Study Unit 32

1 Find the **list** words hidden in this Wordsearch.

T	H	C	R	E	P	C	O	U	H	E	U	K	L
H	R	E	E	P	C	O	U	N	T	C	G	H	N
S	J	O	E	L	A	I	U	N	M	A	I	L	T
F	B	A	T	C	N	L	T	O	V	T	O	L	D
O	A	C	S	T	U	H	M	V	H	A	T	C	H
I	S	S	C	A	L	E	T	E	E	L	O	B	E
T	L	E	T	L	O	A	B	L	G	L	L	C	V
S	T	A	L	K	C	A	B	O	R	L	L	A	W
A	V	I	I	N	R	A	G	U	A	I	B	M	A
S	T	C	L	G	T	G	R	A	T	O	N	H	Y
F	R	P	E	S	C	H	A	T	E	F	D	T	O

And did you mend the broken rail
And make it firm and neat?
I s'pose you want that brindle **steer**
All night among the wheat!
(Henry Lawson)

I must go down to the seas again,
to the lonely sea and the sky,
And all I ask is a tall ship
and a star to **steer** her by.
(John Masefield)

2 Which **list** words?

______________ ______________ ______________

WORD history

Novel comes from the Latin word *novus*, which means new.

Word Knowledge

Which **list** words best fit into these groups?

calf, bullock, heifer ________________

creep, sneak, steal ________________

finger, thumb, wrist ________________

guide, drive, direct ________________

ring, chime, peal ________________

fir, eucalypt, wattle ________________

fare, fee, tariff ________________

stem, trunk, shaft, bole ________________

General Knowledge

1 In the game of poker, does a Royal Flush beat a Full House? ______________

2 What do the following have in common: *Oliver Twist, For the Term of his Natural Life, Gulliver's Travels, Cloudstreet?* ____

3 If you poach an egg do you hatch it, cook it or decorate it? ____________________

Classroom Unit 33 Prefixes

Your List

anticlockwise antiseptic antidote millionaire
millimetre millipede millilitre milligram million
transfer transport transmit transform translate
semi-circle semi-trailer semi-final transparent
periscope perimeter

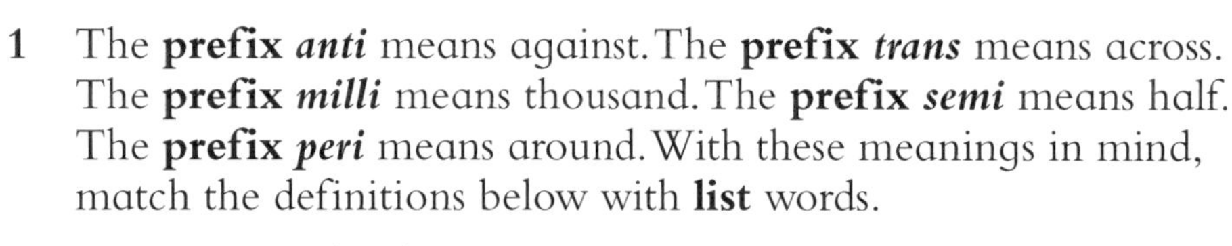

1 The **prefix *anti*** means against. The **prefix *trans*** means across. The **prefix *milli*** means thousand. The **prefix *semi*** means half. The **prefix *peri*** means around. With these meanings in mind, match the definitions below with **list** words.

a creature with what appears to be thousands of legs ________________
something that works against a disease or poison ________________
half a circle ________________
one thousand thousand ________________
an instrument used to look around ________________
the distance around an object ________________
to carry from one place to another ________________
cross from one language to another ________________
one thousandth of a metre ________________
going in the opposite direction of a clock ________________

Strategy

Make word sums.
For example:
antidote = anti + dote
periscope = peri + scope.

2 Write sentences containing the following words.

transform ____
semi-final ____
millilitre ____
antiseptic ____

Word Building

Add the ending shown to each **list** word to form a new word.

transfer (ence) ________________ transmit (er) ________________
transform (er) ________________ translate (ion) ________________
semi-circle (ular) ________________ periscope (ic) ________________
million (aire) ________________ transport (tion) ________________

Challenge

anticlimax antibiotic transistor
peripheral semibreve semi-automatic

Where the wily free-selector walks
in armour-plated pants,
And defies the stings of scorpions,
and the bites of bull-dog ants:
Where the adder and the viper tear
each other by the throat—
There it was that William Johnson
sought his snake-bite antidote.

(A. B. 'Banjo' Paterson)

1 Write the **list** words beginning with ***trans*** in alphabetical order.

____

____

____

2 Write the **list** words beginning with ***milli*** in alphabetical order.

____

____

3 Write **list** words that mean:

to change from one thing to another ______________

a chemical used against germs ______________

one thousandth of a litre ______________

to send out a signal ______________

4 Write the **list** words beginning with ***anti*** in alphabetical order.

____

Word Knowledge

Use a dictionary to find the definitions of the six **challenge** words.

anticlimax ______________________

antibiotic ______________________

transistor ______________________

peripheral ______________________

semibreve ______________________

semi-automatic ______________________

General Knowledge

1 In music, how many crotchets make up a semibreve? ______________

2 How many degrees are there in a semi-circle? ______________

3 What is the perimeter of a rectangle 24 cm long and 10 cm wide? ______________

WORD history

The Latin word *scopium* and the Greek word *skopeo* mean to look at.

How many words can you think of that have come from these words?

Classroom Unit 34

Suffixes

Your List

portable	comfortable	suitable	vegetable	valuable
available	capable	reasonable	remarkable	respectable
responsible	terrible	possible	horrible	
invisible	sensible			percentage
courage	dosage	bandage	carriage	advantage
average	damage	wreckage	marriage	village

Make word sums.
For example:
com + fort + able
in + vis + ible.

1 Write the **list** words ending with ***able*** in alphabetical order.

____

____

2 Adding ***able*** or ***ible*** to a word changes it into an **adjective** (a word that describes a **noun**). The **suffixes** ***able*** and ***ible*** mean ability or likelihood. Complete the following.

A person who is able to reason, is ________________.

Something that is able to provide comfort is ________________.

Someone who is able to use their senses is ________________.

Something that has the ability to cause terror is ________________.

3 The **suffix** ***age*** means a condition or state, or a result. Which **list** words mean…?

the result of a wreck ________________ state of being married ________________

giving medicine in doses ________________ showing bravery ________________

Word Building

1 Add ***ly*** to each of the following **list** words (the ***e*** must be dropped).

comfortable ______________ suitable ______________ terrible ______________

sensible ______________ reasonable ______________ responsible ______________

Select any two of the new words above and write them in one sentence.

____

____

2 Add ***ous*** to each of the following **list** words.

courage ________________ advantage ________________

Write one of these new words in a sentence.

____

Challenge

plumage	mortgage	edible
memorable	audible	divisible

Home Study Unit 34

All for the best in the best of all possible worlds.
(Proverb)

1 Complete the following Wordcrosses using words from the **list**.

Down
1 something that puts you ahead of others

Across
1 able to be used
2 plant used as food
3 having sense
4 having ability
5 bravery

Down
1 showing sound judgement

Across
1 reliable or capable
2 strip of material for wounds
3 ordinary
4 causing horror
5 small town
6 of great value

WORD history

Which of the **list** or **challenge** words come from these Latin origins?
videre—to see
dividere—to cleave or separate

Word Knowledge

Match these word roots with **list** and **challenge** words.

Root	Language	Meaning	List or challenge word
audio	Latin	I hear	audible
portos	Latin	I carry	______
per cent	Latin	in every hundred	______
villa	Latin	country estate	______
carier	French	to carry	______
cor	Latin	of the heart	______
sensus	Latin	of feeling	______
dosis	Greek	to give	______
memorabilus	Latin	bring to mind	______

General Knowledge

1 In tennis, what score comes before Advantage? ______

2 Is a tomato a fruit or a vegetable? ______

3 What percentage of a quantity is three quarters of it? ______

Classroom Unit 35

Compound Words

Your List

fireplace	bushranger	earthquake	whirlpool	grapefruit
sundial	farewell	worthwhile	eyesight	waistcoat
scarecrow	courtyard	toothache	suitcase	blindfold

1 Match the **list** words with the following meanings.

having value ______________ an eye bandage ______________

a dummy to scare birds ______________ area enclosed by buildings ______________

a saying of goodbye ______________ shaking of the Earth's surface ______________

2 These **compound words** are mixed up. Which **list** words are they?

bushquake eyecoat graperanger suitfruit fireache

scaresight toothyard waistcase earthplace courtcrow

____

____

____

Strategy

Make word sums.
For example:
whirl + pool
bush + ranger.

3 Write the following **list** words in sentences to show their meanings.

whirlpool ____

sundial ____

4 Which **list** words might be **antonyms** (opposites) for these…?

worthless ______________ welcome ______________

5 Identify these **list** words.

I contain five **vowels** and five **consonants** and begin with one of the **vowels**. ______________

I contain a double **consonant**. ______________

I contain a double **vowel** and a silent **consonant**. ______________

Word Building

Add words to form **compound words**.

court __ __ __ __ (space enclosed by walls)

bush __ __ __ __ __ (skill at living in the bush)

fire __ __ __ __ __ __ __ (truck for carrying firefighting equipment)

bush __ __ __ __ (forest fire) fire __ __ __ __ __ (fire warning)

fire __ __ __ __ (wood prepared for a fire) fire __ __ __ __ __ (place for a fire)

court __ __ __ __ __ (building where trials etc. are held)

court __ __ __ __ (going out together)

bush __ __ __ __ __ __ (Australian outlaw) fire __ __ __ (gun, rifle, pistol etc.)

Challenge

videotape masterpiece briefcase

Home Study Unit 35

1 Which **list** words?

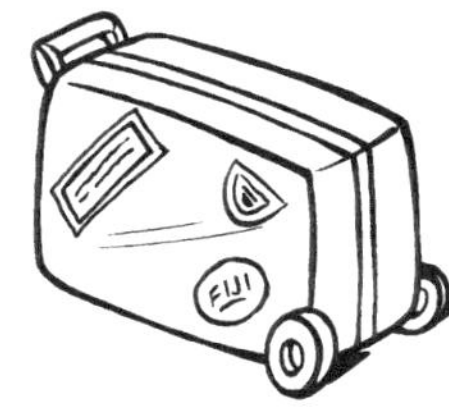

_______________ _______________ _______________ _______________

2 Which **list** words would come between masterpiece and videotape in a dictionary? (Write them in alphabetical order.)

____

3 An **acrostic** sentence, or poem, is one in which the first letter of each word or line spells a word.

For example: earthquake.

Earthquake
Avalanche
Rumbling
Terrifying
Holocaust of
Quaking
Urgency
Awakening all
Kinds of
Emergencies

Choose a **list** word and write your own.

Word Knowledge

Which **list** or **challenge** words are **synonyms** for the following?

valise, handbag, carry-all _______________

outlaw, pirate, brigand, thug _______________

goodbye, au revoir, adios _______________

eddy, vortex, undertow _______________

General Knowledge

1 What does the Richter scale measure? _______________

2 Name the types of people who would deal with the following problems.

a toothache _______________

poor eyesight _______________

a display of masterpieces in a museum _______________

3 Name as many members of the Kelly bushranger gang as you can.

____

Classroom Unit **36** **Contractions**

Your List

I'd	you'd	he'd	she'd	they'd	we're	weren't	aren't
you're	doesn't	isn't	can't	didn't	you'll	it's	

Strategy

The **apostrophe** takes the place of one (or more) missing letters.

1 Match the **contractions** in the **list** with the following:

is not __________ you will __________ it is __________

you had __________ he had __________ does not __________

I would __________ they had __________ we are __________

were not __________ can not __________ did not __________

she had __________ you are __________ I had __________

2 Re-write the following sentences, changing the underlined words to **contractions**.

'You can not have that piece of cake because it is not yours,' sighed Mother.

____

'The train does not pass through this station today,' explained Mr Grimes, the stationmaster.

____

'You had better get a move along if you want to reach the campsite before dark,' called Terry.

____

If you are not the first in line then you will not be the first to be served.

____

3 Write one interesting sentence containing the contractions of did not and they had.

____

4 Write a suitable **list** word in each sentence.

A human __________ see in the dark as well as a cat.

The football players __________ the first onto the field because the umpires had been waiting for several minutes.

'__________ going to the Northern Territory for our holidays,' said an excited Tom.

'You can cook your own tea but __________ have to clean up afterwards.'

Challenge

'twas

Word Building

Write the following **contractions** in full.

didn't __________ doesn't __________ weren't __________

I'd __________ he'd __________ she'd __________

they'd __________ it's __________ can't __________

isn't __________ we're __________ aren't __________

you'd __________ you're __________ you'll __________

Home Study Unit 36

If a thing's worth doing, it's worth doing well.
(Proverb)

1 Write in full the abbreviated words from the proverb at the top of this page.

____

2 Place the **apostrophe** in the correct place in each of these **list** words.

youll	werent	youre	didnt	isnt
theyd	doesnt	hed	cant	youd

3 Write sentences that begin with the following **list** words.

'I'd ______________________________

'You'd ______________________________

It's ______________________________

'Doesn't ______________________________

4 Draw a line from the **list** word to its meaning.

doesn't	we are
I'd	you will
can't	I had
we're	can not
you'd	does not
you'll	you had

WORD history

The contraction *'twas* means it was. We call this contraction archaic, which means that it belongs to an earlier time. You may sometimes find this word still used today in poetry.

5 Draw something that you'd rather not meet.

Word Knowledge

It's and ***its*** are **homophones**. It's is short for 'it is'. Its means belongs to it. On a separate piece of paper, write each word in a sentence to show the difference in meanings.

General Knowledge

1 In the game of soccer, which player isn't penalised for touching the ball with their hands?

____

2 Which of the following birds can't fly? brolga, jabiru, emu, currawong ______________

3 Who didn't die at the Glenrowan seige: Ned Kelly, Dan Kelly, Steve Hart, Joe Byrne?

____

Classroom Review 4

Your List

flour	watch	semi-final	remarkable
flower	antidote	millimetre	impossible
horde	pupil	weren't	flashlight
hoard	postage	breakage	withdraw

1 Circle the correct words in brackets.

A (horde/hoard) of angry people swooped down upon the intruders.

The dragon kept a (horde/hoard) of treasure deep inside the mountain.

(Flour/flower) was used by the chef to thicken the broth.

In the centre of the table, in a beautifully decorated vase, stood a single yellow (flour/flower).

2 The word watch is a **homograph**. Write two sentences that show both meanings of the word.

____

____

3 Find and write the dictionary definitions of:

antidote ______________________________

breakage ______________________________

4 The word pupil is a **homograph**. Write two sentences that show both meanings of the word.

____

____

5 Write in full: weren't. ______________

6 Write in alphabetical order: postage, breakage, impossible, flashlight and remarkable.

____

Word Building

1 Add the ending or beginning shown to each word.

watch (ful) ______________ (un) remarkable ______________

withdraw (al) ______________ impossible (ility) ______________

2 Add *milli* to the following words and then write the definition of each word.

______________ metre ______________________________

______________ litre ______________________________

______________ gram ______________________________

______________ pede ______________________________

Challenge

objectionable spillage greyhound sheer

Home Study Review

> How doth the little busy bee
> Improve each shining hour,
> And gather honey all the day
> From every opening flower!
>
> (Isaac Watts)

Classroom Review 4

1 Find all of the **list** words in this Wordsearch.

```
R W I T H S E M I F I N A L F
E H O R D E W N T L L B L A L
M W O C K G E E E O P O N T A
A A C A Y O R T S W I T U O S
R T A N R O O A S E L O P R H
K C U S W D H W E R E N T P L
A H E M I L L I M E T R E U I
B E E T M I L L I M E T T P G
L I N I M P O S S I B H E I H
E A I M P O S S I B L E R L T
T F B R E A K A G E E F I P L
W I T H D R A W P O S T A G E
```

2 Which **list** words?

______________ ______________ ______________ ______________

Word Knowledge

1 Use a dictionary to find two meanings of sheer.

sheer ____

sheer ____

2 Write each of the following **challenge** words in sentences.

spillage ____

objectionable ____

General Knowledge

1 What do greyhounds chase when racing? ______________________

2 How many millimetres are in…?

one metre ______________ one kilometre ______________

3 Which is usually played first, a semi-final or a preliminary final? ______________

Spelling Reference List

A

abide
abilities
aboard
abrupt
accept
account
accrue
achieve
admire
advantage
advice
affect
afraid
aid
aim
aircraft
alive
allow
allowed
aloud
amount
announce
antibiotic
anticlimax
anticlockwise
antidote
antiseptic
appetite
applaud
apt
aren't
argue
around
arouse
arrive
artichoke
assault
athletics
attempt
attorneys
attract
attune
auburn
audible
audio
audition
August
authentic
autos
autumn
available
avenue
average
avocadoes
awoke

B

baboon
bait
bandage
banjos
barbecue
base
baste
bauxite
beetle
belief
believe
bellow
billow
binoculars
blindfold
bloom
blue
boar
board
bonuses
borrow
bough
bounce
bound
boundary
bout
bow
bowel
bower
break
breakage
breakthrough
breaststroke
breath
breeches
breeze
bridesmaid
brief
briefcase
broke
brood
bruise
buccaneer
buffaloes
buoys
burrow
bushranger
buzzes

C

calves
can't
capable
capsize
cardboard
career
cargoes
carriage
cartoon
case
casualties
cattle
caught
cauliflower
caution
cavities
charities
chase
cheap
cheat
cheese
chief
chimneys
choke
choruses
circuses
claim
clashes
cleat
clothes
clove
cloven
clue
coarse
cockatoos
cocoon
collect
collide
comfortable
commune
compact
concertos
confide
conscript
continue
corps
correct
couch
council
count
counterfeit
country
couple
courage
courageous
courtyard
cousin
cove
coward
cowardice
cower
craft
creature
croon
crouch
cruel
cruise
cuckoos
cue
cupboard

D

daisy
damage
daughter
deaf
death
decide
decoys
deer
deflect
deft
deprive
desire
despite
device
dew
dice
didn't
diesel
dingoes
dinosaur
direct
disease
disrupt
dive

divide
divisible
doesn't
dosage
double
doubloon
doubt
dowel
dowry
doze
drift
drive
droop
drove
drowsy
due
duel
dune
dwarf
dwell
dwindle
dynamite
dynamos

E

eager
eagle
earthquake
easel
easy
echoes
edible
educate
eerie
eight
eighteen
eighth
eighty
eject
elbow
eliminate
embassies
encounter
encourage
engineer
enough
entertain
equinoxes
erase
erect
erupt
exact
except
excesses
exclaim
extinct
extract
eyesight

F

fact
farewell
fast
fate
fault
feather
feature
feeble
feel
fellow
fiascos
field
fiend
fierce
fireplace
fish
flamingo
flamingoes
flashlight
fleece
flour
flourish
flower
flue
foil
folios
foreign
fortresses
fortune
foul
found
foundation
fountain
freeze
freight
froze
fruit
fuel
furrow

G

gait
gauze
geese
glasses
glower
glue
grain
grapefruit
grate
great
Greece
greyhound
grief
grieve
groom
ground
grove
growl
guide

H

halves
handkerchief
harmonies
harnesses
harrow
haste
hatch
haughty
he'd
heap
heathen
heather
heaven
heavy
heel
heifer
heroes
highways
hoard
hoarse
hoary
hoaxes
hollow
horde
horrible
hound
however
hunches
hutches
hygiene

I

I'd
illustrate
imitate
immune
impossible
indexes
inflate
injuries
intercept
invisible
invite
ire
isn't
isolate
issue
it's

J

jealous
jeer
joke
journeys
juice
June

K

kangaroos
keel
kidneys
kilos
kimonos
knead
kneel
knives

L

lagoon
laid
latches
launches
laundries
leashes
leather
leaves
leisure
libraries
lift
lives
loaves
loft
lotteries

lounge
luxuries

M

maid
maim
maize
mangoes
mangrove
manuscript
marriage
marrow
masterpiece
mayonnaise
meadow
meagre
meant
measles
meditate
melodies
memorable
memories
mermaid
milligram
millilitre
millimetre
million
millionaire
millipede
minuses
miseries
misfortune
monsoon
moose
morning
mortgage
mosquitoes
mottoes
mound
mountain
mourning
mouth
mutineer
mysteries

N

narrow
naughty
navigate
needle
neglect
neigh
neighbour
Neptune
niece
nourish
novel
nuisance
nurseries

O

oar
object
objectionable
onslaught
opportune
outside

P

pact
paid
palm
pants
parasite
participate
paste
patches
patios
peasant
peel
peer
penalties
percentage
perfect
perimeter
peripheral
periscope
perspire
phase
pheasant
photos
phrase
pianos
piece
pier
pierce
pike
pillow
pioneer
pleasant
pliers
ploys
plumage
poach
poke
poker
police
polite
portable
possible
postage
potatoes
pouch
pounce
pound
powder
power
praise
precaution
prefixes
presence
presents
priest
princesses
principal
principle
processes
prompt
proof
provide
provoke
prune
pulleys
pupil
pursue
pyjamas

Q

quantities
quantity
quarries
quays
queue
quite

R

raccoon
radios
raft
raid
raise
raisin
ranches
rate
ratios
reap
reason
reasonable
receipt
recesses
recruit
reel
reflect
reign
rein
reindeer
reject
relief
relieve
remarkable
renaissance
reprieve
require
rescue
respect
respectable
responsible
restrict
revenue
retrieve
roar
rodeos
rough
roughneck
round
rove
rue
rune

S

sallow
salmon
sandwich
sandwiches
sapphire
satellite
sauce
saucer
scald
scale
scales
scalp
scan
scar
scarce

scarecrow
scarlet
scatter
scavenger
scene
schedule
scheme
scholar
scholarship
school
schooner
scissors
scold
scone
scoop
scooter
scorch
scorpion
screeches
script
scuba
scurry
searches
season
seen
seethe
select
selves
semi-automatic
semibreve
semi-circle
semi-final
semi-trailer
sensible
separate
shadow
shaft
shallow
shampoo
she'd
sheaf
shears
sheath
sheaves
sheep
sheer
shelves
shield
shift
shire
shower
shriek
siege
site
skate
skateboard
sketches
slate
slaughter
sleeve
sleigh
slice
smoke
smooth
sneer
sneeze
soar
soft
somersault
sopranos
sorrow
sound
sour
south
sparrow
spectacles
speeches
sphinxes
spice
spike
spillage
spire
splash
splendid
splendour
splinter
split
splutter
spoke
spool
squad
squadron
squalid
squash
squat
squatter
squeeze
squid
squirrel
stable
stairs
stalk
stationery
statue
statuesque
steak
steel
steeple
steeplechase
steer
stitches
stoke
stoop
storeys
stout
stove
straight
strait
stretches
strike
strive
stroke
studios
subdue
subside
subways
successes
suffixes
suit
suitable
suitcase
suite
sundial
surround
surveys
survive
swallow
sweat
sweet
swift
switches
swoon
swoop

T

tact
taste
taught
tempos
tempt
terrible
thaw
theatre
their
theory
there
thermometer
they'd
they're
thief
thieves
thirsty
thorax
thorough
thought
threat
throne
thrown
thrushes
Thursday
tissue
to
toadstool
toll
tomatoes
tomorrow
too
toothache
tornadoes
torpedoes
touch
tough
towel
tower
tragedies
transfer
transform
transistor
translate
transmit
transparent
transport
treacherous
treachery
treacle
treason
trios
trolleys
troop
trouble
troublemaker
trousers
trout
trove
trowel

true
tune
tuneful
tuneless
'twas
tweed
tweezers
twelfth
twelve
twenty
twice
twilight
twine
twinge
twinkle
twirl
twist
twitch
two
tycoon
typhoon

U

umpire
universities
uproar

V

vale
valleys
valuable
value
vault
vegetable
veil
vein
veneer
venue
verdict
vetoes
victories
videos
videotape
village
virtue
volcanoes
volleys
volunteer
vowel

W

waist
waistcoat
wallow
waste
watch
we're
weapon
weary
weasel
weather
weigh
weight
weren't
wheedle
wheel
wheelbarrow
wheeze
whenever
whether
whiff
whim
whimsical
whirl
whirlpool
whisk
whisker
whisper
white
wield
willow
window
wirelesses
withdraw
witnesses
wives
woke
wolves
worthwhile
woven
wreath
wreckage
write

X

Y

yield
yoke
you'd
you'll
you're
young
youngster

Z

My Personal Word List

afterwards

therefore

for example

finally

previously

Student Profile

At this level the student's knowledge of:

...is	Not Apparent	Emerging	Consolidating	Established
magic *e* words				
vowel sounds				
ee				
ee_e				
oo				
ou (round)				
ou (double)				
ow (power)				
ow (shadow)				
oa (roar)				
ai (aid)				
ea (heap)				
ea (steak)				
au (caught)				
ei (reign)				
ie (believe)				
ui (juice) *ue* (argue)				
nch				
dge nge rge nce				
ght				
Consonant blends				
sc spl sch squ				
th tw dw wh				
ct ft pt				
Plurals				
s ss sh ch x z				
y to *i* and add *es*				
vowel followed by *y*				
f/fe to *ve* and add *es*				
no change				
always the same				
consonant followed by *o* add *es*				
vowel followed by *o* add *s*				
Homophones				
Homographs				
Prefixes: *anti milli trans semi peri*				
Suffixes: *able ible age*				
Compound words				
Contractions				

Spelling Guide

The English language has grown from many languages so it is difficult to have a set of hard and fast rules for learning to spell.

The following is a guide for spelling rather than a list of spelling rules. Many so-called rules of spelling have exceptions, so it is best to learn the guide and remember the exceptions.

1 To add the suffix ***ing*** to words ending with ***e*** drop the ***e*** then add ***ing***.

For example: skate—skating, dodge—dodging, stare—staring, write—writing.

Exceptions:

If there is a vowel before the last ***e***. For example: seeing, canoeing.

2 To add the suffix ***ing***, ***ed*** or ***er*** to words ending with a consonant, double the consonant.

For example: stir—stirring; span—spanning; plot—plotting; stop—stopped, stopping; travel—traveller, travelling, travelled; run—runner, running.

Exceptions:

- **a** Words ending with a vowel then ***w***. For example: rowed, screwed, chewing, flowing, growing.
- **b** Words ending with a vowel then ***x***. For example: boxer, boxed, boxing, taxed, fixing.
- **c** Words ending with a vowel then ***y***. For example: saying, annoyed, prayer.
- **d** When there are TWO vowels before the last consonant do not double the last letter. For example: repairing, screening, sleeping, squealed, threaded, treated.

3 Put ***i*** before ***e*** when the sound is ***e*** and they do not follow ***c***.

For example: piece, field, believe, achieve.

Exception:

seize

4 Put ***e*** before ***i*** after ***c***.

For example: receive, ceiling, deceive.

Exceptions:

eight, either, neither, height, weight, freight, weird, rein, their

5 *Plurals*

- **a** Words ending in ***s ss sh ch x*** add ***es***.
- **b** Words ending in ***y*** following a consonant, change the ***y*** to ***i*** then add ***es***.
- **c** Words ending in ***y*** following a vowel, add ***s***.
- **d** Words ending in ***f*** or ***fe***, change ***f*** or ***fe*** to ***v*** then add ***es***.

Exceptions:

chiefs, dwarfs, roofs, gulfs, staffs

- **e** Some words have a change of basic spelling.
- **f** Words ending in ***o*** add ***es***. For example: heroes, potatoes, tomatoes.

Exceptions:

Words from languages other than English. For example: pianos, kimonos.

acrostic	a sentence, or poem, in which the first initial of the words, or lines, spell a word
adjective	a word that describes another (for example: tiny dark magnificent)
adverb	words used to tell us more about action and feeling words (verbs) (for example: ran *quickly*, jump *now*, felt *lonely*)
antonym	a word having the opposite meaning to another
apostrophe	(i) a sign showing a letter (or letters) have been left out (')
	(ii) a sign showing that something is owned (for example: Terry's book)
base word	the word from which others may come (for example: circle—circular)
challenge	a group of words that belong to the same family as the list words, but they may be more challenging to master
compound word	a word made up of two words (for example: foot + ball = football)
consonant	letters of the alphabet that are not vowels
consonant blend	two or more letters that are not vowels (*a e i o u*) that make one sound (for example: drum, scream, inspect)
contraction	shortened form of words in which an apostrophe represents missing letters
homograph	a word that is spelt the same as another word but has a different meaning (for example: bear—carry, bear—animal)
homonym	a word that has the same sound or spelling as another word but a different meaning
homophone	two words that sound the same (for example: right, write)
list	a group of words with a similarity in spelling
nouns	words that name something (for example: chair, book, country, house)
onomatopoeia	a word written the same as it sounds (for example: phew)
palindrome	a palindromic word is one that is spelt the same backwards and forwards
past tense	words that say what has happened
plural	a word that means more than one (for example: bunches, boys, foxes)
prefix	a word part that, when placed in front of a word, changes its meaning (for example: interest + *dis* = disinterest)
prime	of the first importance
suffix	a word part that, when added to the end of a word, changes its meaning (for example: happy + *ness* = happiness)
syllable	part of a word that contains a vowel sound or a consonant acting as a vowel (for example: along = a/long)
synonym	a word having a similar meaning to another
verb	a word that tells you about an action (for example: walk, hear)
vowel	the letters *a e i o u*

Spelling Matters—Book 5 (3rd Edition) Answers

Unit	Page	Answers
1	6	**1** phrase baste inflate phase isolate illustrate **2** phase baste slate imitate **3** slate, isolate, inflate rate illustrate **4** chased, pasted, erased, educated, wasted, inflated, imitated, illustrated **WB 1** participation, inflation, imitation, isolation, meditation, elimination **2** wastepaper, tasteless, database, basement, toothpaste, suitcase
1	7	**1** Teacher **2** Teacher **3** Teacher **4** haste, baste **WK 1** meditate, participate, separate, eliminate **2** participate, separate **GK 1** navigate **2** educate **3** suitcase
2	8	**1** sight/site, rite/write/right **2** spice, strike, shire, collide, spire, umpire **3** Teacher **4** slice, umpire, spice, polite **5** admire, arrive, capsize, collide, decide, drive **WB** division, collision, decision, admiration, invitation, provision
2	9	**1** Teacher **2** Teacher **3** pike, perspire, sapphire, ire **WK 1** dynamite, satellite, parasite **2** Teacher (a commonly dull or uninteresting expression; elves/fairies/goblins) **GK 1** Vegemite **2** eat **3** parasite
3	10	**1** cove, doze, grove **2** clove, choke, stove, poke, drove, stoke, froze, mangrove **3** Teacher **4** broke, choke, cove, doze, joke, poke **WB 1** break/breaking/broken, speak/speaking/spoken, wake/waking/woken **2** choking, poking, smoking, stroking, stoking, provoking
3	11	**1** cove *and* love ✗ rove *and* grove ✓ glove *and* stove ✗ doze *and* does ✗ froze *and* toes ✓ doze *and* goes ✓ **2** yolk, yoke **3** provoke/mangrove; broke/choke/smoke/spoke/provoke/stoke/drove/stove/grove/froze **4** Teacher **WK** trove, cloven, woven, artichoke **GK 1** mangrove **2** coke **3** Jove
4	12	**1** immune, June, dune, tune, fortune, commune, misfortune, prune **2** Teacher **3** tuneless/tuneful, fortune/misfortune **4** fortune, immune, June, tune **5** commune, dune, fortune, immune, June, misfortune, prune, tune, tuneful, tuneless **WB** misfortune, fortunate, unfortunate(ly), (un)fortunately
4	13	**1** tune, June, immune **2** Can be found: tune, dune, prune, June, immune *Missing*: fortune, misfortune, tuneless, tuneful, commune **3** dune, June, tuneless, prune **WK** opportunity, immunity, community; opportunity, community, immunity **GK 1** JRR Tolkien **2** prune **3** Neptune
5	14	**1** steer, peer, reel, volunteer, pioneer, engineer **2** feel/eerie, steer/keel, wheel/career **3** deer, steel, peel **WB** cheering, kneeling, peering, sheering, feeling, steering
5	15	**1** sheer, eerie, career, sneer **2** steel, steal, deer, dear, heel, heal, reel, real, peel, peal **3** Teacher **WK** Teacher **GK 1** Rudolph **2** buccaneer **3** mutineer

Spelling Matters—Book 5 (3rd Edition) Answers

Unit	Page	Answers
6	16	**1** Teacher **2** geese/Greece/fleece, cheese/sneeze/freeze/squeeze/breeze/wheeze, sleeve, seethe **3** sleeve/steeple/breeze, wheeze/sneeze (sneeze/wheeze) **4** feeble, see the **WB** sneezing, sneezed, seething, seethed, squeezing, squeezed, wheezing, wheezed
6	17	**1** needle, beetle, steeple, cheese, geese **2** feeble, wheedle, breeze, steeplechase **3** beetle, cheese, fleece **WK** fleece, sneeze, wheeze, breeze, freeze (feeble—with flu) **GK 1** Athens **2** 0° **3** geese
7	18	**1** proof, scoop, shampoo, toadstool **2** smooth, droop **3** bloom, scooter/lagoon/monsoon, croon/swoon, brood **4** toadstool, baboon, cartoon, cocoon, droop, groom **5** Teacher **WB** blooming/bloomed, swooning/swooned, drooping/drooped, swooping/swooped, stooping/stooped, scooping/scooped
7	19	**1** schooner, scoop, scooter, shampoo, smooth, stoop, swoon, swoop **2** droop/scoop/troop/stoop/swoop, brood **3** bloom, typhoon, schooner, tycoon, raccoon, monsoon **WK** swooping eagle, smooth surface, blooming flower, droopy(ing) moustache, crooning singer, scooping spoon **GK 1** papoose **2** schooner **3** troop
8	20	**1** south, boundary, mountain, found, doubt, hound, around, bough, ground, mouth, mound, sound, stout, pound, bound, surrounded, crouch, foul, pounce **2** found, counterfeit, round, sour, stout, aloud **3** couch (lounge), bounce, bough, mound **WB** southwards, accountant, discount, underground, underdog, roundabout, lounge room, doubtful
8	21	**1** Teacher **2** Teacher **WK** Teacher **GK 1** 5 **2** They are all mountains. **3** South
9	22	**1** country, couple, courage, cousin, double, encourage, flourish, nourish, rough, touch, tough, trouble, young **2** Teacher **3** flourish/to grow strongly, nourish/to feed, youngster/a young person, doubloon/an old Spanish coin often stolen by pirates **WB** courageous, troublemaker, youngster, roughneck
9	23	**1** courage, touch, trouble, cousin, encourage, country, double, tough **2** double, couple, courage **3** courage/encourage/courageous, flourish, cousin **WK** Teacher (possible answers—nephew, niece, aunt, uncle, grandfather, grandmother) **WH** courage, encourage, courageous (courage is associated with the heart) **GK 1** Answers may vary: kebabs/Turkey, lasagne/Italy, pita bread/Middle East, goulash/Hungary, souvlaki/Greece, satay/Malaysia, tacos/Mexico, tandoori/India, quiche/France, sushi/Japan, pizza/Italy, chow mein/China **2** courage **3** touch
10	24	**1** allow, bowel, coward, cower, dowel, drowsy, flower, glower, however, powder, power, shower, towel, tower, trowel, vowel **2** flour, aloud, allowed, flower **3** a/u/i/o/e, o/e, o/a/i/e, o/e/e **4** trowel, flower, towel, power, dowel, bowel **5** drowsy, cower, glower, coward, dowry **WB** powerful, powerless, cowardly, cowardice, allowance, however

Spelling Matters—Book 5 (3rd Edition) Answers

Unit	Page	Answers
10	25	**1** *Across:* 1 cower 5 power 6 drowsy *Down:* 1 coward 2 dowry 3 trowel 4 allow **2** Teacher **3** towel, trowel, flower, tower **WK** Teacher (Possible answers: Daisy, Rose, Violet, Petunia, Hyacinth, Iris, Lily, Jasmine, Zinnia, Daphne, Heather, Gladys—Gladiolus, Primrose, Marigold, Poppy, Tulip, Jessamine, Leilani, Iolanthe etc. Possibly also accept: Holly, Ivy, Liana, Laura/Laurel, Fern, Fleur, Flora, Blossom, Myrtle, Olive, Basil **GK 1** London **2** a e i o u **3** blue
11	26	**1** borrow, burrow, furrow, marrow, narrow, sorrow, sparrow, tomorrow, wheelbarrow **2** sorrow, marrow, narrow, willow, hollow, bellow **3** windowsill, shadow boxing, elbow grease **4** Teacher **WB** billowing (Teacher), bellowing (Teacher)
11	27	**1** burrow, swallow, furrow, borrow, hollow, window, meadow, billow, fellow, willow, narrow, elbow, marrow **2** narrow, shallow, borrow, hollow **3** Teacher **WK** harrow, sallow, wallow **GK 1** elbow **2** Teacher (Possible answers: hippo, elephant, pig etc.) **3** marrow
12	28	**1** cardboard, cupboard **2** oar, uproar, boar, roar, hoary, cupboard **3** hoarse, horse course, coarse boar, bore sore, soar bored, board horde, hoard **WB** cupboard, cardboard, uproar, skateboard
12	29	**1** soar, hoarse, hoary, cupboard, uproar, board, coarse, boar **2** aboard, board, cardboard, cupboard, skateboard **3** coarse, hoarse **4** boar, aboard, cupboard **WK** coarsely, hoarsely (Teacher) **GK 1** boar/sow, bull/cow, ram/ewe, buck/doe, stallion/mare, billy-goat/nanny-goat **2** oar **3** hoary
13	30	**1** claim, daisy, praise **2** maim, raise, laid (Teacher) **3** raise, straight, waist, strait **4** Teacher **WB** mislaid, praiseworthy, reclaim, relaid, aimless
13	31	**1** maize, maim, waist, mermaid **2** daisy, raise, maid, maim, mermaid **3** body part between ribs and hips/waist, throw away needlessly/waste, cereal plant/maize, female servant/maid, puzzling pathways/maze, produced/made **4** maize, raisin, mayonnaise **5** praise, laid, paid **WK** exclaim, daisy, gait **GK 1** Hans Christian Andersen **2** Leonardo da Vinci **3** raisins
14	32	**1** Teacher **2** Teacher **3** farmer/sheaf, traitor/treason, chef/knead, biologist/creature (weasel, eagle), artist/easel, ornithologist/eagle **WB** wearily, easily (Teacher)
14	33	**1** Teacher **2** 1 heathen 2 eagle 3 heap 4 easy 5 treacle 6 season **3** knead, wreath eagle, treacle, feature, creature, meagre **4** weary; season; wreath/sheath/cheat/feature/creature/heathen/cleat **WK** sheaf, sheath, knead, need **GK 1** Spring, Summer, Autumn, Winter **2** New Zealand **3** Bering Sea, Sea of Japan, Black Sea, Caspian Sea, South China Sea, Timor Sea, Mediterranean Sea
15	34	**1** break steak **2** grate/great, steak/stake, weather/whether, brake/break **3** sweat, feather, jealous, pleasant, breakthrough, heavy **4** weather, breath, feather, leather **5** heather **WB 1** breakfast, breakthrough, breakneck, breakdown **2** pleasantly (Teacher), heavenly (Teacher), deathly (Teacher)

Spelling Matters—Book 5 (3rd Edition) Answers

Unit	Page	Answers
15	35	**1** Teacher **2** weather, heaven, break, threat **3** steak, sweat, heaven **4** breath, pleasant, death **5** Teacher **WK** green, traitor, hut, scientist, fairy **GK 1** Russia **2** China **3** Charles Dickens
16	36	**1** daughter, applaud, taught, caught, sauce, fault **2** haughty, naughty, vault, slaughter, assault (onslaught), caution **3** dinosaur, vault, saucer **WB** naughtily, haughtily (Teacher)
16	37	**1** Teacher **2** slaughter, saucer, naughty **3** sauce, saucer, slaughter, somersault **WK** audiometer/an instrument for measuring hearing, audiology/the scientific study of hearing, audiovisual/both seen and heard, audiotape/a sound tape-recording, audiophile/one who has great interest in sound reproduction **GK 1** Teacher **2** UFO **3** bauxite
17	38	**1** eighteen, eighty, eighth, eight **2** sleigh, neigh, weigh **3** eight, weight, freight, **4** vein, rein, reign **5** rein/reign, vein, vain, vale/veil, wait/weight, ate/eight **WB 1** reindeer **2** weightless/having no weight, neighbourhood/area in which you live, overweight/weighing too much, leisurely/at an easy pace
17	39	**1** eight, eighteen, eighth, eighty **2** eight, eighteen, eighty **3** heifer, leisure **4** Teacher **WK** veil, heifer, rein, sleigh **GK 1** vein/carries blood to the heart, artery/carries blood away from the heart, aorta/an artery that carries oxygenated blood from the heart, ventricle/heart chamber that pumps blood to the lungs and rest of the body **2** reign, eight, freight, eighty **3** a reindeer might pull or drag a sleigh
18	40	**1** field, fiend, fierce **2** Teacher **3** Teacher **4** Teacher **5** priest, diesel, shriek, hygiene, retrieve, shield **WB** achievement, chieftain, debrief, fiendish, grievance, disbelief
18	41	**1** thief, retrieve, pierce/shield, fierce/shriek **2** beliefs, nieces, thieves, handkerchiefs, chiefs, priests **3** Teacher **WK** verb/grieve, noun/grief, verb/believe, noun/belief **GK 1** father, nephew, mother, aunt, grandmother, brother-in-law, uncle, cousin **2** ship/boat/yacht/ferry/liner etc. **3** priest
19	42	**1** blue, cue, due, flue, bruise, cruise **2** Teacher **3** tissue, glue, fruit (barbecue), juice **4** blue, clue, flue, fruit, fuel, rescue **5** Teacher **WB** argument, valuable, suitable, virtuous, unsuitable, recruitment
19	43	**1** *Across:* 1 barbecue 4 fuel 5 suit 8 rescue 9 glue 10 cue *Down:* 1 bruise 2 rue 3 clue 6 true 7 juice **2** avenue, recruit, cruise, argue, value, duel **3** accrue, venue **WK** issuing, valuing, subduing, arguing, rescuing **GK 1** artichoke, zucchini **2** wine **3** coal, oil, natural gas (petrol) etc.
Review 1	44	**1** fortune, dice, suitable, disease, grain, spool **2** Teacher **3** Teacher **4** enough, suitable, tomorrow **5** meant, white, enough, awoke, skate, sneer **6** a tiny particle/grain, a season/autumn, the day after today/tomorrow, small game cubes/dice, a dairy product/cheese, an illness/disease **WB** believable, tasteful, fortunate, entertainment (Teacher)

Spelling Matters—Book 5 (3rd Edition) Answers

Unit	Page	Answers
Review 1	45	**1** suitable, believe, tomorrow **2** August, pillow/tomorrow, enough/entertain/awoke/around/autumn/August, sneer/cheese/spool **3** Teacher **4** spool, disease, autumn, dice, tomorrow, August **5** white, rough, entertain, autumn **WK** Teacher **GK 1** autumn **2** They are all cheeses. **3** (cereal) grain
20	46	**1** schooner, school, squid, squat, scheme, scar **2** squad, squash, squat, squid **3** scold—to criticise angrily, scald—to hurt or burn with hot liquid **4** squad, scone, splinter, scarce, scald **WB** splitter/splitting, squatter/squatting, scanner/scanning
20	47	**1** Teacher **2** Teacher **3** scuba, squid **WK 1** crab, ant, beetle, rabbit **2** scholar, scuba, squalid, scorpion, splendour, squirrel **GK 1** Robin Hood's Merry Men **2** 3 (Down came the squatters one, two, three!) **3** Scandinavia
21	48	**1** whirl, twirl/twitch **2** twelve/twenty/twelfth, Thursday, twirl, whisker, dwarf **3** twist, dwell, twenty, thaw **4** Teacher **5** No, Yes, No **6** Teacher **WB 1** thoughtful, thoroughfare, bloodthirsty, thoughtless, whenever **2** twinging, dwindling, twitching, thawing, twirling, twisting, whirling
21	49	**1** *Across:* 1 thought 5 whisper 6 dwell 8 twenty 9 twine *Down:* 1 thaw 2 Thursday 3 whisker 4 whirl 7 twist **2** dwell, Thursday, twine/twelve/twinge/dwindle, thought/twilight/twist **3** twinge, twilight, dwindle, whim **WK** Sound: twitter, tweet, whisper Movement: twiddle, twirl, twitch, twist, twinge, whirl, whisk **GK 1** Tweedledee and Tweedledum **2** twelve **3** thermometer
22	50	**1** tempt, lift, prompt, fact, swift, respect, perfect, exact, script **2** pact, collect, attempt, abrupt, respect, loft **3** Teacher **4** attempt, prompt, script, fact **WB** exception, ejection, correction, collection, reflection, objection, perfection, extinction, objection/collection, reflection/ejection, correction
22	51	**1** fact, lift, craft, pact, raft, script **2** soft, swift, correct, reject, tempt **3** collect, reflect, erupt, craft **4** reflect, manuscript, prompt **WK** affection/warm feelings of love, extinction/being wiped out or ceasing to exist, deflection/movement away from something, extraction/taking out, neglect/pay no attention to, verdict/a decision or judgement, disruption/something that throws things out of order, compact/closely packed together **GK 1** They are all extinct. **2** balsa wood **3** Sherlock Holmes
Review 2	52	**1** Teacher **2** tact, tweed, tweezers, twinkle **3** tweed, scalp, apt, squatter, whiff, tact **4** twin/win/wink/ink/in, cave/avenge/avenger, we/wee/weed/(twee) **WB** direction, restriction, interception (Teacher)
Review 2	53	**1** Teacher **2** shaft, twinkle, restrict, splutter *or* squatter **3** shaft, direct, whiff, tact **WK** Teacher **GK 1** Yes **2** Native American Indian (particularly of the Plains' tribes) Native South and Central Africans (and domestic livestock) Inuit (formerly Eskimos) **3** They are all scavengers.
23	54	**1** Teacher **2** hunches, launches, screeches, harnesses, choruses, indexes **3** stretches, thrushes, hoaxes **WB** harnessed, harnessing, harnesses screeched, screeching, screeches stitched, stitching, stitches witnessed, witnessing, witnesses switched, switching, switches

Spelling Matters—Book 5 (3rd Edition) Answers

Unit	Page	Answers
23	55	**1** Teacher **2** switches, patches, launches **WK** wirelesses, minuses, recesses, excesses, processes (Teacher) **GK 1** platypuses **2** walruses
24	56	**1** Teacher **2** Teacher **3** mysteries, lotteries, charities **4** libraries, penalties, nurseries, luxuries **WB** abilities, cavities, melodies, quarries, laundries, quantities
24	57	**1** abilities, tragedies, luxuries, cavities **2** laundries, libraries, lotteries, melodies, mysteries **3** abilities, lotteries, quarries, laundries, libraries, nurseries **4** Teacher **WK 1** Teacher **2** universities, casualties, harmonies, embassies **GK 1** They are all universities. **2** dentist **3** William Shakespeare
25	58	**1** Teacher **2** trolleys, chimneys, pulleys **3** Teacher **4** volleys, decoys, trolleys, valleys, buoys **WB** freeways, subways, highways, causeways, byways, passageways
25	59	**1** *Down*: chimneys *Across*: 1 decoys 2 highways 3 trolleys 4 buoys **2** buoys, quays, storeys **3** Teacher **4** Yes, No, Yes **WK** Teacher **GK 1** three **2** 1 = Princes 31 = Hume **3** valleys
26	60	**1** Teacher **2** thieves, wolves, wives, lives, halves **3** leaves, lives, loaves, wives, wolves **4** knives, shelves, thieves **WB** Teacher
26	61	**1** knives, leaves, thieves, shelves **2** halves, calves, thieves, leaves, shelves, knives **3** Teacher **4** shelves, thieves **WK** Teacher **GK 1** They are all knives. **2** They were all thieves. **3** False
27	62	**1** sheep, fish/salmon/trout or fish/trout/salmon, squid/fish, craft, corps, moose, reindeer or deer **2** corps, salmon **3** trout, craft, reindeer, fish **4** Teacher **5** Teacher **WB** sheep, reindeer, Australian and New Zealand Army Corps
27	63	**1** moose, salmon, corps, trout, squid **2** fish, craft, squid **3** salmon, squid, craft, trout **4** Teacher (stationary) **WK** Teacher **GK 1** one hundred **2** aircraft **3** Teacher
28	64	**1** binoculars, cattle, clothes, glasses, pants, police, pyjamas, scales, scissors, shears, stairs, trousers **2** shears, cattle, glasses **3** pants, stairs, glasses, shears, scales **4** scales, glasses, stairs, scissors **5** Teacher **WB** sunglasses, clothesline, police officer, upstairs, downstairs, nail scissors
28	65	**1** shears, trousers (pants), police, stairs, scales, glasses **2** clothes, binoculars, pyjamas, scissors **3** Teacher **WK** pyjamas, binoculars, breeches (Teacher) **GK 1** binoculars **2** yashmak/Muslim, sarong/Malaysian, Indonesian, sari/Indian, kimono/Japanese, burka/Muslim

Spelling Matters—Book 5 (3rd Edition) Answers

Unit	Page	Answers
29	66	**1** Teacher **2** buffaloes, heroes, mosquitoes, echoes, mottoes, torpedoes, dingoes, cargoes, flamingoes, mangoes **3** tomatoes, potatoes, tornadoes **4** potatoes/tomatoes *or* tomatoes/potatoes, volcanoes, cargoes/torpedoes, mosquitoes/echoes **5** mosquitoes, potatoes, volcanoes, dingoes, buffaloes, flamingoes
29	67	**1** Teacher **2** buffaloes, cargoes, tomatoes, tornadoes, torpedoes **3** Teacher **WK** *echoes*: resonant, ringing, hollow, reverberating, explosive *volcanoes*: violent, furious, fiery, hollow, explosive *heroes*: courageous, gallant, valiant, intrepid **GK 1** torpedoes **2** volcanoes **3** They are both tropical fruits.
30	68	**1** Teacher **2** kimonos, photos, studios, patios, trios, kilos **3** dynamos, sopranos, pianos, folios **4** cuckoos, cockatoos, kangaroos **5** videos, rodeos, radios, banjos, tempos, ratios, dynamos, sopranos **WB** photographs, automobiles, kilograms
30	69	**1** sopranos, rodeos, dynamos **2** autos, folios, photos, trios, videos **3** kimonos, patios, rodeos, cockatoos, pianos **4** Teacher **WK** Teacher (complete and disastrous failures) **GK 1** kimonos **2** librettos **3** cuckoos, cockatoos, taipans
Review 3	70	**1** circuses, hutches, prefixes, princesses, latches, searches, suffixes, successes, clashes, ranches; victories, injuries, memories, kidneys, surveys; shelves, wives; squid, sheep; scissors; tornadoes; radios **WB** submarine, anticlockwise, superstar, report, rewind, cooperate, transport, forehead, unveil, unwind, courageous, comfortable, motorist, successful
Review 3	71	**1** squid, victories **2** sheep, suffixes/successes/scissors/princesses, injuries/tornadoes/victories/memories, kidneys/squid/ranches/hutches/latches/shelves/surveys/scissors/wives/clashes/sheep **3** Teacher **4** kidneys, hutches, suffixes **WK** circum/around, pre/before, milli/thousand, sub/under, trans/across, auto/self, ful/full of, hood/state of being, ist/a person who performs, ship/office or rank **GK 1** kidneys **2** circuses **3** two
31	72	**1** presence/presents, dew/due, allowed/aloud, veil/vale, scene/seen, They're/there/their **2** mourning, bough, throne, morning, bow, thrown **3** Teacher **WB 1** scene, two, principal, allowed **2** weathered, bowed, veiled (Teacher)
31	73	**1** *Down:* principal *Across:* 1 presence 2 weather 3 seen 4 veil 5 allowed **2** Teacher **3** thrown, throne, dew or bow, bough **WK 1** Teacher **2** bough, vale, presents, scene, thrown, due **GK 1** Teacher **2** front/bow, back/stern or aft, left/port, right/starboard **3** Prince Charles (as of 2007)
32	74	**1** toll, scale, count, novel, palm, foil, steer, hatch, novel, stable, palm, count, fast, grate, grate, toll, hatch, stalk, fast, steer, stalk, stable, scale, foil, foil, scale **2** novel, grate, hatch **WB 1** fasten, novelty, discount, full-scale, beanstalk, breakfast **2** Teacher
32	75	**1** Teacher **2** palm, hatch, steer **WK** steer, toll, stalk, palm, palm, toll, steer, stalk **GK 1** Yes **2** They are all novels. **3** Usually you would cook it.
33	76	**1** millipede, antidote, semi-circle, million, periscope, perimeter, transport, translate, millimetre, anticlockwise **2** Teacher **WB** transference, transmitter, transformer, translation, semi-circular, periscopic, millionaire, transportation

Spelling Matters—Book 5 (3rd Edition) Answers

Unit	Page	Answers
33	77	**1** transfer, transform, translate, transmit, transparent, transport **2** milligram, millilitre, millimetre, million, millionaire, millipede **3** transform, antiseptic, millilitre, transmit **4** anticlockwise, antidote, antiseptic **WK** Teacher **GK 1** eight **2** 180 **3** 68 cm
34	78	**1** available, capable, comfortable, portable, reasonable, remarkable, respectable, suitable, valuable, vegetable **2** reasonable, comfortable, sensible, terrible **3** wreckage, marriage, dosage, courage **WB 1** comfortably, suitably, terribly, sensibly, reasonably, responsibly (Teacher) **2** courageous, advantageous (Teacher)
34	79	**1** *Down:* 1 advantage *Across:* 1 available 2 vegetable 3 sensible 4 capable 5 courage *Down:* 1 reasonable *Across:* 1 responsible 2 bandage 3 average 4 horrible 5 village 6 valuable **WK** portable, percentage, village, carriage, courage, sensible, dosage, memorable **GK 1** Deuce **2** fruit **3** 75%
35	80	**1** worthwhile, blindfold, scarecrow, courtyard, farewell, earthquake **2** bushranger, eyesight, grapefruit, suitcase, fireplace, scarecrow, toothache, waistcoat, earthquake, courtyard **3** Teacher **4** worthwhile, farewell **5** earthquake, farewell, whirlpool/ toothache **WB** courtyard, bushcraft, fire engine, bushfire, fire alarm, firewood, fireplace, courthouse, courtship, bushranger, firearm
35	81	**1** fireplace, blindfold, suitcase, scarecrow **2** scarecrow, suitcase, sundial, toothache **3** Teacher **WK** suitcase, bushranger, farewell, whirlpool **GK 1** energy produced by earthquakes **2** a toothache/dentist, poor eyesight/optometrist or optician, masterpieces/curator **3** Ned Kelly, Dan Kelly, Joe Byrne, Steve Hart
36	82	**1** isn't, you'll, it's, you'd, he'd, doesn't, I'd, they'd, we're, weren't, can't, didn't, she'd, you're, I'd **2** can't/it's, doesn't, you'd, you're/won't **3** Teacher **4** can't, weren't, We're, you'll **WB** did not, does not, were not, I would/had, he would/had, she would/had, they would/had, it is, can not, is not, we are, are not, you would/had, you are, you will
36	83	**1** thing is, it is **2** you'll, weren't, you're, didn't isn't, they'd, doesn't, he'd, can't, you'd **3** Teacher **4** doesn't/does not, I'd/I had, can't/can not, we're/we are, you'd/you had, you'll/you will **5** Teacher **WK** Teacher **GK 1** goalkeeper/goalie **2** emu **3** Ned Kelly
Review 4	84	**1** horde, hoard, Flour, flower **2** Teacher **3** Teacher **4** Teacher **5** were not **6** breakage, flashlight, impossible, postage, remarkable **WB 1** watchful, unremarkable, withdrawal, impossibility **2** millimetre–one thousandth of a metre, millilitre–one thousandth of a litre, milligram–one thousandth of a kilogram, millipede–an insect with, seemingly, a thousand legs
Review 4	85	**1** Teacher **2** pupil, pupil, flour, flower **WK 1** Teacher (so thin you can see through it/steep/swerve away) **2** Teacher **GK 1** electronic rabbits **2** one metre/1 000, one kilometre/1000 000 **3** semi-final